The Future of Higher Education

Dan Clawson
Max Page

Higher education is more important than ever, for individual success and for national economic growth. And yet higher education in the United States is in crisis: public funding has been in free fall; tuition has skyrocketed making colleges and universities less accessible; basic structures such as tenure are under assault. *The Future of Higher Education* analyzes the crisis in higher education, describing how a dominant, neo-liberal political ideology has significantly changed the U.S. system of higher education. The book examines the contemporary landscape of higher education institutions and asks and answers these questions: Who is able to attend college? Who pays for our system of higher education? Who works at and who governs colleges and universities? The book concludes with a plan for radically revitalizing higher education in the United States.

Dan Clawson is Professor of Sociology at the University of Massachusetts Amherst, and the author or editor (sometimes with others) of seven books and numerous articles, including *Public Sociology* (2007) and *The Next Upsurge: Labor and the New Social Movements* (2003). He is a former president of the UMass faculty union and serves on the board of the statewide Massachusetts Teachers Association.

Max Page is Professor of Architecture and History at the University of Massachusetts Amherst. He is the author of *The Creative Destruction of Manhattan* (1999) and *The City's End* (2008), is a former president of the Massachusetts Society of Professors, the faculty and librarian union at UMass Amherst, and serves on the Executive Committee of the 110,000-member Massachusetts Teachers Association.

University Readers
Reading Materials Evolved.

THE SOCIAL ISSUES COLLECTION™

Routledge
Taylor & Francis Group

Framing 21st Century Social Issues

The goal of this new, unique Series is to offer readable, teachable "thinking frames" on today's social problems and social issues by leading scholars. These are available for view on http://routledge.custom gateway.com/routledge-social-issues.html.

For instructors teaching a wide range of courses in the social sciences, the Routledge *Social Issues Collection* now offers the best of both worlds: originally written short texts that provide "overviews" to important social issues *as well as* teachable excerpts from larger works previously published by Routledge and other presses.

As an instructor, click to the website to view the library and decide how to build your custom anthology and which thinking frames to assign. Students can choose to receive the assigned materials in print and/or electronic formats at an affordable price.

Body Problems
Running and Living Long in a Fast-Food
Society
Ben Agger

Sex, Drugs, and Death
Addressing Youth Problems in American
Society
Tammy Anderson

The Stupidity Epidemic
Worrying About Students, Schools, and
America's Future
Joel Best

Empire Versus Democracy
The Triumph of Corporate and Military
Power
Carl Boggs

Contentious Identities
Ethnic, Religious, and Nationalist Conflicts in
Today's World
Daniel Chirot

The Future of Higher Education
Dan Clawson and Max Page

Waste and Consumption
Capitalism, the Environment, and the Life of
Things
Simonetta Falasca-Zamponi

Rapid Climate Change
Causes, Consequences, and Solutions
Scott G. McNall

The Problem of Emotions in Societies
Jonathan H. Turner

Outsourcing the Womb
Race, Class, and Gestational Surrogacy in a
Global Market
France Winddance Twine

Changing Times for Black Professionals
Adia Harvey Wingfield

Why Nations Go to War
A Sociology of Military Conflict
Mark Worrell

The Future of Higher Education

Dan Clawson
Max Page
University of Massachusetts, Amherst

Routledge
Taylor & Francis Group

NEW YORK AND LONDON

First published 2011
by Routledge
270 Madison Avenue, New York, NY 10016

Simultaneously published in the UK
by Routledge
2 Park Square, Milton Park, Abingdon, Oxon OX14 4RN

Routledge is an imprint of the Taylor & Francis Group, an informa business

© 2011 Taylor & Francis

Typeset in Garamond and Gill Sans by EvS Communication Networx, Inc.

The rights of Dan Clawson and Max Page to be identified
as authors of this work have been asserted by them in accordance with
sections 77 and 78 of the Copyright, Designs and Patents Act 1988

Library of Congress Cataloging in Publication Data
Clawson, Dan.
The future of higher education / Dan Clawson, Max Page.
p. cm. — (Framing 21st century social issues)
Includes bibliographical references.
1. Education, Higher. 2. Universities and colleges. I. Page, Max. II. Title.
LB2325.C594 2011
378—dc22
2010028383

ISBN13: 978-0-415-89206-3 (pbk)
ISBN13: 978-0-203-83418-3 (ebk)

Contents

Series Foreword   vii

Preface and Acknowledgments   ix

I. Introduction   1

II. The Lay of the Land   8

III. Who Governs the University?   15

IV. Who Pays?   23

V. Who Goes?   31

VI. Who Works?   38

VII. Choosing a Future   45

References   54

Glossary/Index   58

Series Foreword

The world in the early 21st century is beset with problems—a troubled economy, global warming, oil spills, religious and national conflict, poverty, HIV, health problems associated with sedentary lifestyles. Virtually no nation is exempt, and everyone, even in affluent countries, feels the impact of these global issues.

Since its inception in the 19th century, sociology has been the academic discipline dedicated to analyzing social problems. It is still so today. Sociologists offer not only diagnoses; they glimpse solutions, which they then offer to policy makers and citizens who work for a better world. Sociology played a major role in the civil rights movement during the 1960s in helping us to understand racial inequalities and prejudice, and it can play a major role today as we grapple with old and new issues.

This series builds on the giants of sociology, such as Weber, Durkheim, Marx, Parsons, Mills. It uses their frames, and newer ones, to focus on particular issues of contemporary concern. These books are about the nuts and bolts of social problems, but they are equally about the frames through which we analyze these problems. It is clear by now that there is no single correct way to view the world, but only paradigms, models, which function as lenses through which we peer. For example, in analyzing oil spills and environmental pollution, we can use a frame that views such outcomes as unfortunate results of a reasonable effort to harvest fossil fuels. "Drill, baby, drill" sometimes involves certain costs as pipelines rupture and oil spews forth. Or we could analyze these environmental crises as inevitable outcomes of our effort to dominate nature in the interest of profit. The first frame would solve oil spills with better environmental protection measures and clean-ups, while the second frame would attempt to prevent them altogether, perhaps shifting away from the use of petroleum and natural gas and toward alternative energies that are "green."

These books introduce various frames such as these for viewing social problems. They also highlight debates between social scientists who frame problems differently. The books suggest solutions, both on the macro and micro levels. That is, they suggest what new policies might entail, and they also identify ways in which people, from the ground level, can work toward a better world, changing themselves and their lives and families and providing models of change for others.

Readers do not need an extensive background in academic sociology to benefit from these books. Each book is student-friendly in that we provide glossaries of terms for the uninitiated that are keyed to bolded terms in the text. Each chapter ends with questions for further thought and discussion. The level of each book is accessible to undergraduate students, even as these books offer sophisticated and innovative analyses.

Clawson and Page in their book for this series offer a highly original discussion of the present status and future of American higher education. They certainly know the academic world well! They discuss various models of academic life and they situate their analysis in the real-world context of today's economy, which is very challenging both to tuition-paying students and to those who must run universities on an increasingly tight budget. The authors bemoan the business model that, they contend, increasingly dominates the administrative cultures of American universities. But they do not only criticize current practices in higher education; they end their book with suggestions for sweeping change.

Preface and Acknowledgments

Higher education is more important than ever, for individual success and for national economic growth. And yet higher education in the United States is in crisis: public funding has been in free fall; tuition has skyrocketed making colleges and universities less accessible; basic structures such as tenure are under assault. *The Future of Higher Education* analyzes the crisis in higher education, describing how a dominant, neoliberal political ideology has significantly changed the U.S. system of higher education. This book examines the contemporary landscape of higher education institutions and asks and answers these questions: Who is able to attend college? Who pays for our system of higher education? Who works at and who governs colleges and universities? The book concludes with a plan for radically revitalizing higher education in the United States.

Books and courses should be about more than facts and concepts taken in the abstract; the purpose is not only to learn about the world, but to change it. The system of higher education that we have was shaped by powerful actors pushing an agenda that we fiercely oppose. One "small" decision after another, often made "reluctantly", has re-shaped higher education. Collectively we have the power and the capacity to create a new system, one which serves the interests of *all* the people—but it will only happen if people like the readers of this book join a mass movement to build a new and better system of higher education. We are part of such an effort, and thank all those who have joined with us in that struggle to oppose the decline of public higher education—including activists everywhere, especially at UMass and in PHENOM (The Public Higher Education Network of Massachusetts). We thank as well those who provided helpful comments and inspiration along the way—Mary Ann Clawson, Nancy Folbre, Naomi Gerstel, Eve Weinbaum, Ferd Wulkan, and Robert Zussman.

1:   Introduction

In a time of fractious political debates, there seems to be a consensus on this: Every American needs a college education.

Just look at what leaders at the opposite end of the political spectrum say. Here is Deval Patrick, Governor of Massachusetts, former Clinton Justice Department official, and close friend of President Obama: "Success in a 21st century global economy requires more than a high school diploma." And Margaret Spellings, George W. Bush's Secretary of Education: "What a high-school diploma was in the '50s is akin, more and more, to at least two years of postsecondary education today" (Basken 2008). And here is President Obama's challenge to the Congress:

> I ask every American to commit to at least one year or more of higher education or career training … we will provide the support necessary for all young Americans to complete college and meet a new goal: By 2020, America will once again have the highest proportion of college graduates in the world.

With this kind of support, one would think that the future of higher education is bright. In fact, higher education in the United States is in the midst of a major crisis, of funding, affordability, mission, and organization. A nation which once had a higher education system that was the envy of the world has, in a few short decades, weakened the quality of its institutions of higher learning, and lessened their accessibility by students of all racial, ethnic, and class groups. Other nations, most notably China and other growing nations in Asia and the Middle East, are investing huge sums in creating public universities and broadening access.

This book will introduce you to some of the central debates raging about the future of higher education in the United States. Who can and should attend college? What is the purpose of a college education? Who should pay for it, and how much? Who should govern the modern university? How has our system of higher education come to the point of such a crisis? (There are many debates we don't get into, but are of great importance as well: What should colleges teach? What is the role of political debate in the life of colleges and universities?)

You may have immediate answers to these questions: anyone who is smart should be able to go to college if they work hard and save up; the purpose of a college education is to get a good job; students and their families should pay, with a little help from the government; universities are businesses like any other and should be run as such;

tough economic times require belt tightening everywhere, which is why colleges are hurting.

In some situations, "trusting your instincts" is good advice. But not in college. Our goal is to get you to acknowledge your instinctual answers, and then challenge them with new facts and new perspectives. In short, we want you to develop a "sociological imagination" that will help you develop an understanding of the issue at hand—the future of higher education—but also develop a way of thinking that can be applied to every other social issue that you as a student and citizen wrestle with.

The Sociological Imagination

The most famous work of American sociology is C. Wright Mills' (1959) *The Sociological Imagination*, written 50 years ago. Mills argued that those who acquire the **sociological imagination** "come to feel as if suddenly awakened … They acquire a new way of thinking." This way of thinking "is the capacity to range from the most impersonal and remote transformations to the most intimate features of the human self—and to see the relations between the two." The sociological imagination helps people to understand the relations between "personal troubles" and "public issues of social structure" and as such "the sociological imagination [is] our most needed quality of mind."

This book provides concrete facts and examples of what is happening to *The Future of Higher Education*, but we hope that it does more: that it gives you an example of what it means to apply the sociological imagination to a problem that shapes the future of our society. We desperately need a 21st century sociological imagination that can be applied both to an analysis of personal lives and to broad historical transformations. Do brains, ability, and hard work explain why some people have no trouble getting into one of the nation's most selective colleges, and graduate debt-free in four years, while others struggle to make it to college at all, take six years to graduate, and leave with debt up to their eyeballs such that they can't afford to take a public interest job? To what degree do these outcomes depend on the characteristics of the individual and to what degree do they depend on the place in which those individuals find themselves in a larger **social structure**? If students are failing to graduate from college in a timely manner, is this because students today just aren't as smart and hard-working as they were in the old days, or is it because public higher education has been systematically deprived of funding, with students forced to pay many thousands of dollars a year by working many hours for tuition money?

In today's world, a sociological imagination is central to understanding the diversity of experience of people, depending on their race, gender, class, and sexuality. We cannot understand our own biographies, or larger historical and structural processes, without a rich and deep understanding of the ways these factors shape our lives, even if—perhaps especially if—these forces are largely invisible to us and to others.

The sociological imagination demands that we walk a two-way street, between individual choice, or "**agency**," and social structures which shape our actions. The sociological imagination is not, as the name might imply, a question of imagination in the abstract. That imagination must be grounded in evidence, evidence which may take a range of forms from examples and stories to systematic assessments and quantitative analyses. Facts must be given meaning and significance by becoming parts of larger arguments.

We hope to have you replace your received "instincts" with the will to engage in the questioning that is central to the sociological imagination.

A Brief History

Every society has ways of helping young people learn what they need to know to become fully functioning adult members of the society, but it is not written in the stars that a society has to do so through schools, much less that those schools need to be provided by the government and be free to all residents of the society. The notion of universal free education—at least for some number of years—is a very new idea in the history of the world. Two hundred years ago, most children in the United States spent relatively little time in schools of any sort, and very few of the children in school were in free public schools. The Founding Fathers held education in high esteem and believed that only an educated citizenry would be able to sustain this new invention—a republic governed by its citizens. But for much of the 18th and 19th centuries, formal schooling was limited to young white men, and only those of the wealthier classes. The public school movement, pioneered by Horace Mann of Massachusetts, changed that. By 1900, virtually every community provided free public schools at least through eighth grade; in the early 1900s the high school movement made free public high schools universally available, and over time in most states students were required to attend school until at least age 16.

Colleges and universities have been a part of the United States almost since Europeans settled here; Harvard University was founded in 1636 and all but one of the Ivy League schools were founded before the American Revolution. Most of these early universities were created to train ministers for the diverse churches of the young and relatively religious colonies. Only slowly did they develop into training grounds for leaders of civic and business life. Most of the 18th and early 19th century colleges were created with private funds, along with public support and approval. In 1800 there were only 23 colleges in the young nation; a century later there would be 821. The primary impetus for this growth came in 1862. As part of the progressive Republican Party agenda, the Congress passed the Morrill Act, which allotted some 30,000 acres of federal land to each state and required them to house a new public college or university on the land, and use the proceeds from the sale of the rest to pay the expenses of operating the newly created institutions. These so-called "land-grant" public colleges and universities are the basis for the public higher education system we have today. Most "flagship" campuses in each state—like Ohio State University, University of Wisconsin, and our own University of Massachusetts—began as Morrill land-grant universities.

Public colleges and universities expanded relatively slowly, but were an established part of the landscape in the late 19th and early 20th century United States. They were not designed to serve large numbers of students; there was no expectation like the one President Obama articulated. Rather, these universities were designed especially to support the economic and public life of the state—for example, training farmers on the latest approaches to agriculture at the Massachusetts Agricultural College (which would only become UMass Amherst 80 years later), or devising patents to improve dairy production at the University of Wisconsin. As public institutions gained momentum—with the rise of the Progressive era (1900–20) and its emphasis on scientific research and public solutions to societal problems—more students attended colleges and universities, and more of them attended public institutions. By 1940, the balance between public and private institutions was roughly equal.

There was, however, a dramatic shift after World War II. With the continued growth in white-collar jobs that demanded higher education, a GI Bill that gave returning veterans fully paid college educations, and the rapid baby boom that would expand the number of college-age students in the 1960s, the number of college students more than doubled in the dozen years from 1963 to 1975, increasing by 134.0 percent (National Center for Education Statistics 2010: Table 190). In the following 33 years, to 2008, enrollment increased by only half as much (by 70.8 percent) as in the earlier, much briefer period, reaching a total of 19.1 million. During the 1960s, growth was concentrated in the public sector; since then growth has been much more rapid among private colleges and universities, as funding for public institutions has declined (see Chapter IV). In the 1963–75 period, the public sector grew more than four times as fast as the private sector (186.8 percent public, 38.4 percent private); in the 1975–2008 period, the private sector grew twice as fast as the public sector (118.3 percent private, 58.1 percent public).

Many consider the period of the 1950s and 1960s the "golden age" of higher education in the United States, because in this era the United States built the world's finest system of public and private universities and this system drove the growing economy, spurred technological advance and innovation in every major industry, led to improvements in public health, and spurred the outpouring of art, literature, theater, and film. Furthermore, in this period, colleges and universities became more broadly accessible than ever before, fulfilling a century-old dream.

It is no accident that the era of the United States' greatest economic and cultural growth, from the end of World War II to the early 1970s, corresponded so perfectly to the era of the greatest investment in higher education, and especially public higher education.

Neo-Liberalism: In Society and in Higher Education

The growth of public investment in higher education roughly paralleled the rise of a post-New Deal consensus that government—and especially the federal government—could and should play a central role not only in spurring economic growth, but in providing essential services for the American citizenry—housing, health, a safe, clean environment, and education. That consensus always had its detractors, and they grew in numbers and volume as government expanded its reach. A growing conservative movement in the 1960s and 1970s would finally take control of the federal government with the election of Ronald Reagan in 1980. That conservative, or **neo-liberal**, message dominated Congress, the White House, and the general tenor of public debate for the next quarter century, up to the present.

This book focuses mostly on the changes in higher education that have taken place since about 1980. Conservatives came in many stripes, but found their own consensus: a deeply held belief in the power of markets to generate economic growth, and a virulent hatred of federal government action in virtually any sphere. In Ronald Reagan's 1981 inaugural address, he argued that "Government is not the solution to our problem; government *is* the problem." If government is the problem, then we should be cutting back on what the government does. Conservative activist Grover Norquist provided a memorable, and oft-quoted, formulation: "My goal is to cut government in half in twenty-five years, to get it down to the size where we can drown it in the bathtub."

Perhaps the most effective way to reach this long-term goal is to reduce taxes, so the government has less money to spend. The initial conservative claim, by both Reagan and his economic advisors, was that cutting taxes would stimulate so much economic growth that the deficit would not go up. That turned out not to be the case, and the supposed fiscal conservative Reagan ran up massive budget deficits, deficits that continued under his successor, the first President Bush. Government deficits themselves became a means of enacting the conservative agenda of reducing the size of government. Although the tax cuts were sold on the basis that they would not increase the deficit, when they in fact increased the deficit there was no move to raise taxes; instead conservatives intensified their pressure for more cuts in government. Those budget deficits were then inherited by President Clinton, who spent much of his eight years in office reducing the deficits of the Reagan and Bush (the first) era instead of expanding government programs. In effect his presidency became a means of bailing out the Republicans, who had run up large deficits in order to provide massive tax cuts for the wealthy. The second President Bush then introduced a further tax cut for the wealthy, turning Clinton's budget surpluses into new record deficits. When President Obama came into office these deficits were used as an argument about why no further expansion of government programs should be undertaken. An additional element of this political consensus is that military spending is sacrosanct—no significant force pushes for cuts in military spending. An anti-tax and pro-military spending consensus produces an inevitable next step: a perpetual squeeze on domestic programs.

Despite important differences at the margins, today these tax-cutting, government-shrinking policies are in effect accepted by both Democrats and Republicans; that is, there is a de facto consensus, at both the national and state levels, to accept neo-liberal policies. Even when President Obama and the Democrats passed health care reform, over strong Republican opposition, the bill was required to pay for itself, and be a means of reducing the deficit. Democrats as well as Republicans are far more likely to run on a platform of reducing taxes than on a platform of introducing significant new government programs. This is true at the national level, but perhaps is even more so at the state level where most of the funding for public higher education comes from.

These tax-cutting, government-shrinking policies are part of a larger ideology called neo-liberalism, which holds not only that government is bad, but also that the "free market" is the best way of addressing pretty much any social problem. If an industry is regulated, it should be de-regulated, with the various companies in the industry competing with each other to hold down costs. If a service is provided by the government, it should be **privatized**, that is, turned over to a for-profit business. In this view, the federal health care program for older people, Medicare, should be replaced by private health insurance companies. If an institution—say a college or university—has been hiring its own groundskeepers and gardeners, that work should be contracted out, with the existing employees replaced by the contractor's employees.

In a great many cases, the result of these neo-liberal practices is to lay off full-time employees with decent pay and benefits, and replace them with much lowerpaid workers receiving few if any benefits. The workers who are laid off might be unionized workers in the United States; their replacements might be highly exploited $3-a-day workers in China. College groundskeepers earning $18 an hour with pensions and health care might be replaced by (undocumented) immigrants earning $9 an hour with no benefits. In other cases—say, the financial industry, which was freed from many New Deal-era regulations in the 1980s and 1990s—the deregulation leads to dramatic collapses, as bankers and investors engage in riskier and riskier, and unregulated, gambles with other people's money. When economic disaster hits—as it has frequently and with growing size in the past two decades—the government is then used to bail out the industry for its mistakes. Those who made the big mistakes, and made the big bucks, don't have to pay for their errors—the taxpayers do, while the top executives continue to get many millions (often many tens of millions) in bonuses, despite their catastrophic mistakes. The neo-liberal ideology is so strong that, despite the colossal collapse of the de-regulated finance industry, despite a government bailout requiring literally trillions of dollars, the ideology of weak regulation in the service of the "free market" continues its dominance.

We will argue that neo-liberal policies are similarly problematic for universities. For many years U.S. higher education was the envy of the world—we provided college education to more students than any other country in the world, had a large percentage of the world's top-ranked universities, and were a magnet for the very best students from around the world, who often stayed, becoming leaders in their field. Under the last 30 years of neo-liberal policies, those U.S. advantages have been eroded.

The next five chapters explore the contours of a system of higher education as it has been reshaped by the neo-liberal ideology. In Chapter II we provide some basic information about how public higher education is organized in the United States. In Chapter III, we ask the simple but important question: Who runs the university? We look at three different models for university governance, and their impact on the nature of colleges and universities. Chapters IV and V describe how dramatically financing for colleges and universities has changed, and how this has affected who attends. We describe a system that has turned away from public funding and has reversed the trend of broader access. Chapter VI describes how the neo-liberal approach has affected academic workers—faculty and staff who do the work of the university. In Chapter VII, we come clean, and offer for debate our vision of a different higher education system, one that is a reverse image of the neo-liberal society that we largely live in today.

DISCUSSION QUESTIONS

1. Why did you go to college? Why did your friends?
2. Why did your parents want (or not want) you to go to college?
3. Why are colleges and universities important, or unimportant, to the larger society?
4. To what extent do your answers to the first three questions mesh, and to what extent do they contradict each other? That is, did you go to college for the same reasons your parents wanted you to go, and for the same reasons society supports colleges and universities? If the answers are different, what sorts of conflicts, if any, does this cause between the individual and the society?

II: The Lay of the Land

❧⚬❧

Sarah, 18, just received her admission letter to Yale. She is excited about the next four years of academic and extracurricular activities. She has a strong interest in political science but has no firm idea about what kind of career she wants. She is eager to sample the variety of courses at Yale and figure out what she wants to major in. Already, she is looking forward to a semester abroad in Paris, and to summer internships in New York.

Jon was admitted to the undergraduate business degree program at the University of Nebraska. He grew up in Omaha and expects to spend his life in his home state. With his parents' support, he will attend full-time and live in a campus dorm. However, because of work and the difficulty of getting into required classes at this huge public university, he knows (based on the experience of his friends) that it will likely take him five or six years to graduate.

Paul is working while pursuing a two-year degree in law enforcement at Berkshire Community College in Massachusetts, but hopes eventually to get a bachelor's degree. He has signed up for three courses this term, but expects that with work he will have to drop at least one and maybe two. He is fortunate that many of the courses are offered in the evening, as his work for the census bureau during this census year requires him to work during the day.

Kim works full-time as a secretary at a hospital in rural Missouri. There are no nearby colleges for her to fulfill her dream of becoming a paralegal. She recently enrolled in a degree program with Kaplan University, a for-profit university that offers classes online. Although it costs more than a community college, she doesn't have to drive the 50 miles to get there, and she can "attend" class at any time—from her computer.

So, who is the typical college student?

Short answer to a complicated question: Today it is Paul. Yesterday, it might have been Jon. It was never Sarah. Tomorrow, it might be Kim. Full-time, public university college students dominated the landscape in the 1960s and 1970s. Students at the elite private universities have always been a small percentage of the total college-bound student body. And in the future, those who attend college by booting up their computer may well be the majority.

In this chapter we offer a view of the higher education landscape today.

Higher education is a major part of our society. The more than 18 million students are served by more than 3.6 million employees (National Center for Education

Statistics 2010: Table 187). The number of college students is greater than the number of chief executives, financial officers, claims adjusters, accountants and auditors, computer programmers, architects, social workers, lawyers, paralegals and legal assistants, librarians, athletes and coaches (and umpires and related workers), photographers, chiropractors, dentists, veterinarians, Emergency Medical Technicians and paramedics, firefighters, police, cooks, bartenders, waiters and waitresses, electricians, and plumbers and pipefitters combined (U.S. Census Bureau 2009: Tables 269, 103).

These numbers also mean that a large percentage of the population enrolls in college. Of those who complete high school, more than two out of three (67.2 percent) enroll in college (U.S. Census Bureau 2009: Table 267), although as we will discuss in Chapter V, many of these people will not complete college, certainly not within four or five or six years. Most of our attention will be on undergraduate education and institutions, but increasingly people feel the need for education beyond the bachelor's degree. There are 2.7 million students in some form of post-baccalaureate education. A slight majority (54 percent) are full-time, and about six in ten (59 percent) are women.

Much of the discussion of higher education, however, centers not on where most of the people are, but instead the very top institutions—eight Ivy League universities, a dozen liberal arts colleges, and (depending on the topic) maybe a half-dozen flagship public universities. Those institutions obviously matter, and they educate a disproportionate number of our nation's elite, but the huge numbers of students are to be found elsewhere. The Ivy League universities enroll only 56,859 undergraduates; the top ten liberal arts colleges (places like Amherst, Williams, and Swarthmore) have less than 30,000 students. Together the undergraduates at those top institutions have only one-half of 1 percent of all students (that is, 1 out of every 200 college students).

Five points help provide a framework for thinking about college students today.

The beginning point is that almost three out of four college and university students (73.9 percent, to be precise) are in public institutions; only one out of four (26.1 percent) attends any form of private institution—Ivy League university, Christian college, small liberal arts college (U.S. Census Bureau 2009: Table 269). Those public universities include places like the University of California Berkeley, which is arguably the best research university to be found anywhere in the world, but they also contain many state colleges and community colleges. The latter schools attract relatively few of the rich and famous, but they provide millions of students with a first-rate education. They used to do so at a very affordable price—virtually free in California and New York—but increasingly they are being financially squeezed, raising tuition and fees in response.

The second point is that more than a third of total college enrollments are at these two-year institutions, which generally means community colleges (U.S. Census Bureau 2009: Table 269). Because students need only two years in community colleges, but four years to get a bachelor's degree, the fact that more than a third of enrollments are at community colleges is an indication of the fact that at least since 1980, "the majority of all degree-credit students entering the system of higher education have done so in a two-year institution" (Brint and Karabel 1989: v).

A third point to keep in mind when trying to form a mental map of higher education is that well over a third of students (38.2 percent) are part-time, not full-time (U.S. Census Bureau 2009: Table 269). Many of them are working to support themselves, or raising children, or taking care of sick parents, or all of these, while also attending college. The image of a student with a backpack walking down a tree-lined avenue surrounded by Gothic buildings represents the experience of only a small minority of American college students.

The fourth orienting point is that students come in all ages. A majority of students are traditional-aged students, that is, no more than 24 years old. That accounts for a bit more than six out of every ten students (61.8 percent), but almost 7 million students are older than that, including 1.9 million students aged 40 or more (National Center for Education Statistics 2010: Table 192).

A fifth and final point is that there is a new and rapidly growing sector in higher education: For-profit colleges and universities. For much of our history, virtually all colleges and universities—public and private—have been non-profit. Even though many private universities are wealthy, they are officially not-for-profit institutions. But in the past decade, the growth of for-profit universities has exploded. The largest university in the nation is not Ohio State or the University of Texas—it is the University of Phoenix, with 400,000 students. Although the University of Phoenix has its name emblazoned on the Peter Eisenman-designed football stadium near Phoenix, there is no University of Phoenix football team because, although it has buildings in many states, there is no University of Phoenix campus in any traditional sense. It, along with many other for-profit universities, does most of its business online. It is estimated that 10 percent of all college students in the United States are enrolled at for-profit universities.

There are good reasons for the growth in on-line education: for-profit universities answer the desperate need for flexible scheduling that is the result of the increase in work hours, single-parent families, and two-earner families, making the possibility of pursuing a college degree that much more difficult. The results can be seen in the numbers: The University of Phoenix's parent company, the Apollo Group, reported a rise of 22 percent in enrollments between 2008 and 2009. In particular its two-year degree program—the associate's degree that has traditionally been offered by community colleges—grew by 37 percent in that same period (Eduventures 2010).

Its profits grew as well—27 percent in that same year—and this has only added to the growing chorus of critics. The University of Phoenix gets more federal financial aid money than any other university (and the next four highest financial aid recipients are also for-profit universities), even though it has low graduation rates (16 percent, one of the lowest of any university in the nation), low success in placing students in other universities, offers a curriculum that many argue is inferior, and which is taught by an underpaid and underqualified faculty (Dillon 2007).

Traditional, "bricks and mortar" colleges and universities are responding rapidly to the challenge from for-profit universities by offering a growing number of courses online, both as a way to respond to real needs, and to raise more money for their traditional programs. The funding crisis (which we discuss in Chapter IV) has led the vast majority of all public universities (along with a majority of private universities) to offer online courses and degrees (National Center for Education Statistics 2008).

Although there are a comparative handful of colleges only for women, and a larger number of Historically Black Colleges and Universities (which are open to white students, but continue to enroll overwhelmingly black student bodies), the most striking differences between schools are based on class; as a rough rule (with some exceptions), the more prestigious the institution, the more affluent the student body.

Clearly, it can be deceptive to talk about the "typical" college experience. Let's look in a little greater detail at four types of "bricks and mortar" colleges and universities: Harvard, a most competitive university; the University of Massachusetts Amherst (UMass), a flagship public university; Pikeville College, a non-competitive private college; and Holyoke Community College (HCC). Two of these schools are private (Harvard, Pikeville) and two are public (UMass, HCC). Attending any of them is "going to college," but what this means and what the experience involves can differ substantially. There is a dramatic class divide separating Harvard at the top, UMass and Pikeville in the middle, and Holyoke Community College at the low end.

Harvard, founded in 1636 and based in Cambridge, Massachusetts, is across the river from Boston, on a beautiful campus with many historic buildings. The University of Massachusetts Amherst, the state's flagship public university, founded in 1863, is in the small town of Amherst in a semi-rural area. The campus is pleasant but hardly luxurious; although there is one new upscale dorm, and some new buildings, much of the physical plant is aging and most of the dorms are utilitarian. Pikeville College, with 800 students, was founded in 1889 by the Presbyterian Church and is a private institution in the eastern Kentucky hills, about 20 miles from Virginia and 30 miles from West Virginia. Holyoke Community College is on the mall-outskirts of town on the edge of Holyoke, Massachusetts, a 50,000-resident declining former factory town. Most of its quite pleasant campus consists of a set of three inter-connected buildings surrounded by parking lots.

Much of the discussion of colleges focuses on how selective they are, with the implication that all colleges are similar to Harvard, the most selective school in the country. Out of every 100 applicants, Harvard accepts fewer than eight; of those who are accepted, more than three out of four enroll. UMass Amherst is somewhat selective, but not remotely as selective as Harvard; UMass actually had more applicants than Harvard (29,000 to 27,000), accepting two out of every three applicants, with only one in five of those accepted actually enrolling. While "selectivity" is the catchword at some of the wealthiest and most elite private colleges, in fact many colleges and universities in the United States have essentially "open admission." Pikeville College admitted 100 percent of the 2007–08 applicants, and that is also the policy of Holyoke Community College.

These differences in selectivity are associated with differences in students' grades and test scores. Although tests scores are a highly problematic indicator, and are strongly correlated with a student's family income (Owen 1985), they offer a way to make basic comparisons. At Harvard, three out of four of those admitted have **SAT** scores over 690 on the critical reading test. At UMass Amherst, on the same test, only one out of four students have scores over 630, so the test scores for a student at the upper fourth of UMass's students aren't as good as those for a student at the bottom fourth of Harvard's students. Even though it admits everyone, Pikeville requires that students take and submit test scores on the **ACT**. In the freshman class, almost six out of ten students had scores that would put them below 515 on the critical reading SAT test. (Fewer than one out of four UMass students have scores that low, so the bottom quarter of UMass is at about the same place as the top third of Pikeville.) Most Holyoke Community College students have never taken the SAT or ACT test; many of them don't know what these tests are, and don't need them to attend the college.

The selectivity of admissions and the income the campuses can count on per student are associated with big differences in the chances that students will graduate, or indeed even return for a second year. At Harvard, almost everyone—97 out of 100—graduates in four years. At UMass Amherst, the great majority of students (87 of 100) return for a second year, but only half (49 of 100) graduate within four years, and only 66 of 100 graduate within six years. At Pikeville, most of those who enter (51 of 100) will not be back for their second year, and only 30 of 100 will graduate. At Holyoke Community College, half the students are part-time, many raising families and working long hours, and know from the beginning that they will be stretching their college experience over many years.

Whether a student attends Harvard, UMass Amherst, Pikeville, or Holyoke Community College, they are attending college. But these experiences are very different. Despite the efforts to broaden access (which we discuss in Chapter V), Harvard students are from the elite. Many of them come from the wealthiest families—about half of all Harvard students have family incomes above $180,000 a year, four times the national average (Inside Higher Ed 2007)—and for the most part they went to the best high schools and prep schools, and had terrific grades and test scores. Almost all will live on campus and few will put in significant work hours while in college. They will spend four years associating with other members of the elite from all over the country and the world, and they will go on to hold key positions of power in every important part of American society. At the other end, Holyoke Community College students won't live on campus, will mostly attend college while also working, many full-time or nearly so, many raising families. They will be in class primarily with students from within 30 miles of the school, many of whom struggled in high school. For most, their college education will enable a modest promotion or boost in income. Holyoke Community College has a good record at placing a handful—but only a handful—of its two-year graduates at elite area colleges, and once in a while a Harvard student may end up washing dishes, but both outcomes are exceptional. Many schools aspire to be more like Harvard than they now are, but the future of higher education, and of the kind of society we hope to create, rests in what happens to flagship public universities and community colleges.

The kind of school we aspire to create is related to our thinking about why students do, and should, attend college. People attend college for many different reasons. For some it is almost unthinking: everyone around them always assumed they would do so. For many it is among other things a chance to party, drink, ingest assorted drugs, and have sexual encounters. College can be a time of freedom, an opportunity to make friends for a lifetime, and a chance to explore ideas, meet different kinds of people, and see the world in new ways.

Much of the discussion of college today treats it as an economic investment that is expected to pay off in higher lifetime earnings. And it does: a college degree—any college degree—is likely to increase one's income. Comparing the median incomes of people with differing amounts of education, on average, earning an associate's degree increases a person's income by $8,245 a year (from $33,801 for a high school graduate to $42,046 for someone with an associate's). Going on to get a bachelor's degree adds another $13,610 (for an income of $55,656), and a master's ($67,337), doctorate ($91,920), or professional ($100,000) degree further raises income (Current Population Survey 2009: PINC-03). Put another way, getting a four-year bachelor's degree can nearly double one's yearly income; getting a professional degree—like a law or business degree—can triple it. These represent massive changes in life earnings and financial stability.

It makes a lot of sense for individuals and society to give as many people access to an education and a credential that will allow them to live a life of relative financial stability. But lost in this emphasis—which has become dominant only in the past generation—are all the other benefits of a college education and experience for the individual and, ultimately, society. College graduates are more likely to stay married, less likely to commit crimes, more likely to vote, less likely to smoke, and more likely to volunteer. All of these represent benefits to the quality of life of the individual, but also generate a better society—more taxes paid, a stronger democracy, fewer health costs, a richer culture (Watts 2001). Harder to measure, but no less important, is that a college education can expose people to new ideas and help them think in new ways.

In the next chapter we show how there has been a sea change in how universities are governed, which mirrors the changes in why students attend college, and what society hopes to get out of those college graduates.

DISCUSSION QUESTIONS

1. Where does the school you attend(ed) fall on various measures of its social position and the character of its students?
2. To what extent, and in what ways, does that make it "typical" or a-typical?
3. To what extent do these measures capture something significant about your school, and what do they miss?
4. When people think of "going to college," what image does that evoke? How much difference does it make—in terms of the experience while in school, in terms of the outcomes for later life—what sort of school you go to?
5. To what extent do you think students at your school (at other schools) are attending college because they believe it will boost their income, and to what extent are students there for other reasons?

III: Who Governs the University?

I n our daily lives, we take a great deal for granted. We assume that most children will be brought up in families, not in orphanages; that most schools and most classrooms will contain both boys and girls, rather than having boy-only and girl-only schools; that we will cover our bodies, or at least strategic parts of them, with clothing, even if it is hot in the summer; that if you don't work you won't get paid (unless you work on Wall Street); that you can't vote or buy liquor until you reach the legal age (18 for voting, 21 for liquor), and a whole host of other things.

In the same way, we take for granted that we know what is meant by a college or university, and that we know how it functions. We know that there is a president or chancellor and provost up at the top somewhere; that below them there are a bunch of deans of various sorts; that there are academic departments, each with a department head or chair; that there are faculty who teach classes; that each class is worth a certain number of credits; that students get grades; that the grade (supposedly) reflects how much work the student did and how much he or she learned; that a certain number of credits are needed to graduate; that a college degree is the needed proof you went to college and learned something; and so on.

Put another way, there are certain institutions and structures in place, backed by a set of cultural understandings and taken-for-granted assumptions that make it easy for us to function. When it comes to college and university, we know what is meant and we know how things will operate. We do *not* question everything. Social structures are powerful mechanisms for channeling our behavior.

One of those things we don't usually think about is how the governance of a university is related to the mission of the university. Or, in other words: what are universities for and how should they be governed to realize these goals?

In some ways, universities look very much as they have for over a century; in some respects—like caps and gowns and residential quadrangles and faculty lectures—today's colleges would be recognizable by a student at Oxford University in England in 1450. Much of what it means to be a college or university is not currently being contested (although it might be a good thing if people *did* challenge some of those assumptions). But some parts of what it means to be a university, and how a university should be run, are very much in contention. Colleges and universities, especially but by no means exclusively public colleges and universities, have been and are being fundamentally transformed. Often people don't see the larger picture, and think only about one or another specific change (or battle), but in this chapter we would like to step back and look at the larger contest.

This chapter contrasts two models of what a university or college is and how it should be run—the university as an institution dominated by professionalism and faculty governance, and the university as a business. In Chapter VII, we will discuss a third possibility—the university as a democratic institution run by all those involved in it. Forty years ago, professionalism and faculty governance dominated colleges and universities, and a radical student movement sometimes challenged that with a vision of the university as a democratic institution. Today, colleges and universities are increasingly run as businesses, with faculty fighting a generally losing battle to preserve professionalism and faculty governance.

Professionalism and Faculty Governance

Through much of the 20th century, after the birth of the modern and secular university, most institutions of higher education were run on a model based on the concept of **professionalism** and **faculty governance**.

Professionalism operates on the basis of people who are educated to develop both expertise and a set of values and commitments (Brint 1994; Freidson 2001; Larson 1977). Professionals—such as faculty—treat each other as peers and are accorded a considerable degree of self-governance. The idea of professionalism is that professionals cannot be properly evaluated by those from the outside, and that professionals can and should be trusted to evaluate and police themselves, operating not on the basis of self-interest but rather with a vision of some larger good.

Consider **tenure**, which is both the most important structural mechanism providing protection for professionalism and faculty governance, and is also an example of faculty control of a key aspect of the university. The decision on who will receive tenure depends almost entirely on the judgment of other faculty. In a faculty member's sixth year on the job, other faculty make a decision as to whether the candidate's performance is strong enough to merit the award of tenure. If the answer is yes, the faculty member is more or less guaranteed a position for the rest of their lifetime; if the answer is no, the faculty member is fired, even if he or she has been doing a perfectly fine job. Scholarship, teaching, and service all matter in the decision of whether or not to award tenure, but at research universities by far the most important criterion is scholarship. A good teacher who did not publish articles and books, or conduct scientific research, or create innovative new art or theater work, would not win tenure. Although administrators and the Board of Trustees in theory have the final say on whether or not someone is awarded tenure, at most good universities, administrators and trustees almost always ratify the decision made by the faculty.

Tenure is not an absolute guarantee of a job—a faculty member who harasses students, or has sexual relationships with students, or uses drugs, or commits a felony, can and will be fired. But tenure offers very strong protection—almost, but not quite, a guarantee—that a faculty member will not be fired for taking unpopular positions, disagreeing with other faculty, or publicly arguing that the chancellor is ruining the university.

In the faculty governance model, the assumption is not that the student knows best. Rather than responding to student/consumer preferences—which may be shaped by the latest fad or trend—the faculty should guide, advise, and mentor students. Students should be required to take courses they would not otherwise choose—the science major to read Shakespeare, the English major to study astronomy.

Similarly, in this model administrators do not know best; faculty do. Since only a fully-qualified professional could evaluate other professionals, at most universities, in order to be a dean, provost, or president, a person must qualify as a tenured member of the faculty. Ideally administrators should be promoted from the ranks of the faculty (and, at a later point, return to the faculty), not brought in as outsiders (Tuchman 2009). The iconic figure is not the administrator hopping from place to place and going up the academic prestige hierarchy, but rather the faculty member who has stayed for a lifetime and serves as a symbol of the college. The venerated administrator is not the person who increased revenues the most, but rather the person who took a stand on principle and refused to bend to pressure from above, resigning if necessary to uphold a principle. The goal is not short-term success in rankings, but integrity and standing for basic values for the long run.

In a way, it was quite a radical notion: The core employees—the teachers and researchers—make the decisions about who to hire into their ranks, who to keep, what courses—call them products if you like—to offer, and how to evaluate people and programs. The administrative employees—the president or chancellor and his or her staff—are structurally removed from some of the most important decisions of the university. They serve the faculty rather than the other way around.

This very unbusinesslike notion is derived from the university's long-understood mission as a place of free discovery and communication of knowledge, and a belief that the mission was too important to leave to anyone but those professionals committed to it.

The faculty governance model has been, and continues to be, a powerful ideal for many universities. At its best it relies on and in turn helps to create faculty acting on deep-seated principles who have a long-run commitment to the college and to its values (a passionate pursuit of truth, a commitment to nurturing students and helping them develop, a defense of free speech and freedom of research, a dedication to decisions based on long-run collective values rather than short-run self-interest). When the system works well, faculty fight hard to defend the university against attack, whether by outsiders or by short-sighted administrators, and protect the university as a sanctuary from the pressures and rewards of the outside world.

And that is the essential point: the model of a university governed by professionals is one that consciously segregates financial concerns from academic decisions. No doubt, the line has always been fuzzy, but it was understood to be there: we use money to achieve an intellectual and teaching mission, not the other way around.

That has begun to change, and rapidly.

The University as a Business

Fifty years ago almost no one talked in terms of a college or university as being like a business, but today this is unequivocally the dominant model. Because neo-liberalism dominates the larger society, every major institution is under pressure to run itself in terms of market mechanisms, governance structures, and ways of thinking.

We do not mean to suggest that all colleges and universities now seek to make profit for investors, although as we discussed in Chapter II, an increasing number of students attend universities which exist to do exactly that, where educating citizens and expanding knowledge are purely secondary. Rather, the business model in higher education makes the following demands: the university must generate its own funds to keep itself solvent, and the university must therefore structure all of its activities— its governance, its reward system for faculty, its recruitment of students—around the mission of raising funds for its operation.

We are in the midst of a transition—which we hope will be resisted—from the faculty governance model to the business model. Therefore, other than the for-profit universities, there are no pure examples of universities run on the business model. There are many long-standing structures—such as a Faculty Senate that approves courses and programs—that remain at most non-profit universities. But everywhere, the change has set in, insidiously, we believe.

If a college or university is a business, or at least should be run like one, then the chancellor or president should be like the Chief Executive Officer (CEO) of a company; when he or she gives orders, they should be obeyed right down the line. (Indeed, an increasing number of university presidents are being recruited from the business world.) Just as middle managers have little or no say over how a corporation is run, the faculty should have minimal influence in running a university. Like any manager, they can offer their thoughts and suggestions, but it is up to the CEO and the Board to decide.

In this business model, students are the consumers, but they are also in some sense the product. The most democratic way of running things, according to the business model, is a free market which responds to consumers. Consumers, including student consumers, go to the market every day and "vote" for the products they want. The college should respond to these student choices, re-shaping the curriculum to meet what students want today. Because the faculty are likely to resist such changes, there needs to be strong leadership from the top.

As in any marketplace, some consumers have more money than others, and businesses need to be most responsive to those with money to spend. A student who needs financial aid brings in fewer resources, and is therefore less valuable, and the institution should do less to attract such people. (Because there are opposing pressures—coming from legislatures, for example, in the case of public universities, it is rarely stated this baldly, and small but highly visible gestures are made in the direction of access.) The most affluent students want a fancy gym and luxurious dorms; state universities should make those a priority in order to attract out-of-state students (who pay higher tuition). The student whose parents might be able to make a substantial donation to the university is even more valuable; such a student should be admitted even if she or he is dumb as a post and mean as a snake. If out-of-state students pay $10,000 a year more than in-state students (and often the difference is more than that), then if the university can replace 100 in-state students with 100 out-of-state students, the university administration gains $1 million a year; roughly the same logic applies to replacing financial-aid students with full-paying students. One final statistic says it all: In 2003, the big public research universities spent $171 million on financial aid for families at the bottom of the income scale. But they spent $257 million on financial aid for students from families that earn more than $100,000 per year (Folbre 2010: 60) (an income which is about double the average family, and puts them into the top fifth of all families). Slowly and steadily, the university is shifting its investment toward the higher yielding crop.

If the university is a business, then the more money it generates the better it is doing, and anyone or anything that brings in money is to be valued over anyone or anything that costs the university money. Thus, if a faculty member brings in external grant money, he or she is increasing the university's revenue and making a valuable contribution. In theory the grant money is all to be spent on the research for the grant, so there isn't money left over as a "profit" to the university, but if a university brings in grant money that definitely raises the university's and the chancellor's prestige.

A faculty member who does a different kind of research, on a topic or for a group that won't lead to grant funding, is—by this logic—less valuable. What research is more likely to get an outside group to provide external support—research showing that toxic waste dumps aren't really a problem, or research on how poor people can stop toxic waste dumps from being located in their neighborhoods? The group with money is the corporation looking to dump toxic waste, and it might find it useful to have a university study showing toxic waste dumps aren't a problem; poor people have no money, so research on stopping toxic waste dumps is much less likely to be funded. Does that mean that the university should honor the pro toxic-waste dump researcher, and neglect or penalize the anti-toxic-waste dump researcher? Although business-model administrators would try hard to avoid such a question, in practice their answer is "yes."

This bottom-line orientation is even more evident when it comes to the question of patents, or research which might conceivably result in something that could be patented. This is a dramatic change from an earlier practice.

> In 1955, when newscaster Edward R. Murrow asked Jonas Salk who owned the patent to his polio vaccine, he famously replied, "Well, the people, I would say. There is no patent. Could you patent the sun?" Harvard, Chicago, Yale, Johns Hopkins, and Columbia all had policies on the books that explicitly forbade patenting of biomedical research.
>
> (Washburn 2005: 52)

The Bayh-Dole Act of 1980, little noticed or contested at the time, made it possible for universities to patent inventions and knowledge that resulted solely or in part from federal funding. It's worth stressing what that means: The federal government provides the money to do the research, but the researcher, the university, and even more so a private corporation make the money off the invention. Consider Taxol, the best-selling cancer drug of all time, with over $9 billion in sales. "All of the research on the drug was conducted at, or supported by, the National Cancer Institute," but nonetheless "the government paid Bristol-Myers Squibb hundreds of millions of dollars for Taxol through the Medicare program" (Angell 2004: 58, 66).

Consider the University of California Berkeley as an example of what this can mean. In 1998, the College of Natural Resources struck a deal with Novartis that, in exchange for $25 million, gave Novartis first rights to a substantial fraction of university research and required faculty to sign confidentiality pledges. As one California state senator pointed out, if faculty came upon results that indicated a danger to the public, it appeared that faculty would be forbidden to disclose that information without permission from Novartis (Washburn, 2005). Similarly, in the fall of 2007 Berkeley signed a $500 million pact with BP for a Research Institute that gave BP first shot at much university research, and where much of the research was to be confidential with results entirely owned by BP. One way of looking at it is that a part of Berkeley has become a partially owned subsidiary of BP. In that situation, in the 2010 BP oil spill, were Berkeley faculty experts free to speak out on the issue? As a more general process, if a university has a choice between freely and immediately sharing the results of its research—the foundation for scientific knowledge, and necessary for the process of replication—or withholding results in the hopes of winning a valuable patent, what will the choice be? Patent income is by no means trivial: nationally, for all universities combined, income from patents brings in more than $1 billion a year (Blumenstyk 2007).

Part of this university-as-a-business model is that where markets do not exist, efforts should be made to create pseudo-markets, and then to use those to behave as if there were a true market. Internal allocations within a campus are increasingly driven by rating systems and so-called "benchmarking." National rankings in places such as *The Princeton Review; U.S. News and World Report, Newsweek's* Top 100 Global Universities, and the Association of American Universities are used as measures of an institution's quality. Departments are required to produce standardized data so that administrators can assess their "quality" as compared with departments on other campuses. Benchmarks as a form of pseudo-market are used to force departments to compete against each other, with rewards (for example, permission to hire new faculty) going to those departments that score highest. Just like a market system, the aim is to create winners and losers, increasing the stratification within the university. This is combined with a system that gives top administrators increased control over all aspects of faculty hiring. Hiring decisions were once made almost entirely by the faculty in the department concerned; now those decisions must be reviewed and approved by those at the top, and often the decision is de facto made at the top.

If the university is a business, then the top executives (administrators) are clearly much more important to the success of the institution than are the faculty. And in fact we find that over the last decade or more, administrators have consistently raised their own salaries more than faculty salaries; sometimes there is a relatively small difference, sometimes a dramatic difference. Related to this, administrators are not loyal to a particular institution; rather, they come in, introduce a handful of changes that will build their résumé, then move on. The average tenure of a provost is 5.2 years and of a president 8.5 years (American Council on Education 2008), but many faculty spend their entire careers at one institution, and are fiercely loyal to it.

To be fair, many boards of trustees, chancellors, and deans insist that they are trying to defend the traditional university's mission of teaching, research, and service and only adopt the business model because costs have risen and funding—especially for public universities—has declined at an unprecedented rate. All of this is true, as will be discussed at length in the next chapter. What these well-meaning (some, at least) administrators fail to understand is that the traditional idea of a university—which has produced much of what we understand to be modern civilization—cannot survive the business model.

The implications of a business model are felt and seen everywhere and, if unchecked, will take over even those areas of the university that still today remain from a generation ago, and seem sacred. In the future, we may see pre- and post-tests for college students, so that we can quantify what students have learned. In the future, faculty may no longer have ownership of their class notes and syllabi, but will see them replicated in online courses taught by adjunct faculty thousands of miles away. The idea that faculty are more than vehicles for delivering information to students will promote head-scratching. And the very notion of "going to college" will seem like a luxury, unnecessary for the acquisition of a degree, which will now be delivered electronically and not at a passé tradition called "Commencement."

In the following three chapters, we explore in greater depth the implications of the business model in higher education, as we look at who pays for our colleges and universities, who gets to attend them, and how our colleges and universities treat the millions of workers who run them.

DISCUSSION QUESTIONS

1. How is your college or university governed? If you don't really know, what are the implications of that?
2. In what ways, if any, do you see your college or university being run like a business, or refusing to be run like a business?
3. Do you think that, for students, it makes any difference how the college or university is run? Do students care?
4. How much influence do students have in how the university is run? Is it at the level of "we can pick the band for the spring concert" or do students have a significant influence on decisions about costs, courses, and priorities?

IV: Who Pays?

Who pays for college? There are a number of choices—parents, students, states, the federal government, private foundations and endowments.

But you might ask the following: Who cares? Obviously, students and their parents do, because if it is them (as it increasingly is), they are likely to be burdened with years if not decades of debt. We want to argue here that all of us—college students, faculty, but also regular citizens—should care who is paying for our colleges and universities, especially the public ones that serve three out of four students. We show in this chapter that there has been a fundamental shift in how education is funded, with an increasing share of the costs borne by students and their families, and a rapidly decreasing amount paid for by states and the federal government.

We have alluded to this shift in previous chapters, but we want to emphasize here that it is perhaps the most fundamental shift in American higher education in 50 years. Neo-liberalism wants to shrink government, and to make government answer to the logic of the market. That includes reducing state funding of higher education. This is what led to the adoption of the business model. It is what has led to the shifting of costs to parents. It is what has made it that much harder to fulfill the American promise (already under strain) of social mobility. It is what has led to the declining pay and benefits of the millions of workers on college campuses. It is what ultimately threatens academic integrity and the quality of teaching and research. For higher education, the most powerful tool of that ideology has been to stop the flow of public dollars to colleges and universities.

So who does pay?

First up are the students and their families, for whom costs keep escalating. For the most expensive private colleges, the costs are astronomical. For example, Harvard's tuition and fees in 2009 were $36,173; the full cost of attending (including room, board, books and other supplies) pushes beyond $50,000 per year. The other colleges we discussed in Chapter II are much cheaper, but still represent a huge expense for the average family. UMass Amherst's tuition and fees add up to $11,732 for an in-state student (and $23,229 for an out-of-state student). Although Pikeville College is much less selective than UMass Amherst, its tuition of $15,250 is substantially above what an in-state student pays at UMass. Holyoke Community College is the bargain here, costing only $3,072.

Part of the shock of those numbers is simply the amount, especially when compared to the average household income of $50,303 in 2008 (Current Population Reports 2009: 5–6). But another part comes from the change over time.

If you had gone to an average public four-year university in 1970–71, you would have paid $428 in tuition; in 2010 dollars that would be $2,401 for tuition (National Center for Education Statistics 2010: Table 334).

The most recent figures in the *Digest of Educational Statistics* are those for 2008–09. Unfortunately those are woefully out of date—costs have been skyrocketing since—but by those data, the 2008–09 tuition for an average public university, in 2010 dollars, was $7,712. That is, *after adjusting for inflation,* tuition more than tripled (up 3.2 times) from 1970–71 to 2008–09.

If tuition at an average public university today cost $2,401 we would obviously have a very different situation. A student doing a job at the federal minimum wage could earn that much with 331 hours of work, that is, about 10 hours a week for 33 weeks. In other words, with no help from their parents and no financial aid a student could pay their full tuition simply by working 10 hours a week from the beginning of September to the end of April, with two weeks off for Christmas; then they could take the summer to earn money for books, room, and board. If that seems ridiculous, remember that this actually *was* the situation in 1970–71. Students could put themselves through college, and graduate debt free. (Note that in inflation-adjusted terms, the 1970–71 minimum wage was more than $8.00 an hour, higher than today's $7.25.)

The bottom line is this: where once public higher education was affordable, today it represents an ever-growing strain on families and on students. As we discuss in Chapter V, it has made a substantial difference in who gains the benefits of college.

Because a college or university is most obviously about students and teachers, if students are paying dramatically more, it would be easy to conclude that the reason must be that faculty are getting big raises.

That's not at all the case. If tuition had increased at the same rate as tenure-system faculty salaries, what would the 2008–09 tuition have been at an average public university? Tuition would have increased from $2,401 all the way up to $2,504. Clearly faculty salaries are *not* the reason for rising tuition costs.

Since this result is so counter-intuitive, it's worth taking a more detailed look at faculty salaries over this same time period of 1970–71 to 2008–09. Salaries for full professors went up by 2.7 percent, but salaries went down for associate professors (by 2.4 percent) and assistant professors (by 0.8 percent) (National Center for Education Statistics 2010: Table 257). Because colleges and universities have not been doing much hiring lately (at least not of tenure-system faculty), the mix of faculty has changed—there are fewer assistant professors and more full professors—and since full professors earn substantially more than assistant professors, overall faculty salaries have increased by 4.3 percent. And these are salaries for full-time workers; as we will discuss in Chapter VI, full-time tenure-system faculty are increasingly being replaced by part-time and adjunct faculty who are paid a fraction of what full-time faculty earn.

True, there are stories of individual faculty members making hundreds of thousands of dollars, especially in scientific disciplines and at medical schools. And the very wealthiest private universities pay well. The average full professor makes $192,000 at Harvard, for example. But those numbers drop quickly when we look at public universities and small private universities. At UMass Amherst, the average full professor—that is, a person at or near the top of their field, with at least 15 years of teaching and writing, and acclaim from their colleagues around the country—earns $117,000. Just down the road, at Holyoke Community College, the numbers are only a bit over half that—$66,000. And at Pikeville, the Kentucky college we discussed in Chapter II, an average full professor makes just above the national average family income amount—$56,000 (American Association of University Professors 2010).

If faculty salaries aren't what is driving the rapidly escalating cost of colleges and universities, what is? We suggest at least four factors: The importance of a college education gives institutions market power to increase costs; the increased inequality in incomes means that the affluent can afford to pay high costs; the university-as-business model itself leads to a competition for and emphasis on the most affluent students; and most important, the decrease in government support for affordable public higher education. Let's look at each of those four factors.

College–University Market Power

A college education, as we discussed in Chapter II, has a big impact on your future earnings, the jobs you get (and don't get), the networks you form, the friends you make, your standing in the world, and so much more. Many people believe in the following scenario: College A will cost you $5,000 a year more, but will *probably* put you in a significantly stronger position for your later life; College B is okay but might end up costing you the good job you hoped for at 25 and the promotion you hoped for at 40. Faced with this choice, most people will do their best to go to College A if they possibly can. Students want College A, and parents want their children to be able to go to College A even if it costs the parents an extra $20,000 over the student's college career. Much as in health care (this doctor's a pretty good cancer surgeon, this doctor's the best cancer surgeon), people see the choice as incredibly important and (if they can afford it, as many can) aren't that price sensitive. Students and parents will pay more to get a better school, schools know this, and so can charge more if they can make a claim of higher quality. The truth of this choice is a lot less clear than people believe (Dale and Krueger 2002), but the belief holds.

Increased Inequality

Not everyone goes to college. The top end of the college spectrum, the most selective private colleges and universities, are attended and funded disproportionately by those at the top end of the income distribution. In the last 30 years, incomes have stagnated for most of the population, but they have increased dramatically for the top 10 percent and even more so for the top 1 percent—tripling or even quadrupling. Those are the people most likely to go to Harvard, and most likely to donate to Harvard, and those people have had enough money that rapidly rising tuition is not much of a problem for them. We will discuss the issue of inequality and who gets to attend college in Chapter V.

The University-as-Business Model Itself

If colleges and universities are to be run like businesses, what constitutes the measure of success? For a business it is profits and stockholder value, but what is it for a college? There is no clear uniform answer to this, but the two most likely indicators are the institution's total revenues and, even more so, the institution's prestige. For research universities, one important measure of revenue is the dollar amount of the research grants received. For all schools, an important indicator is likely to be the level of donations and the size of the increase in the endowment.

Prestige is measured above all by the national rankings put out by various magazines and, especially for undergraduate institutions, the (measurable) quality of the student body. Magazine rankings may use dubious methodology and problematic indicators, but students and parents take them seriously, and institutions tie themselves in knots to move up (or avoid moving down) in the rankings. In assessing the quality of the student body, the easy, quantifiable, supposedly neutral measure that is available to people is the SAT test, and average SAT scores are probably the most widely used indicator. We can imagine university presidents standing around saying "My SAT's bigger than yours is." SAT scores are highly correlated with class and income, so much so that the College Board tried to prevent researchers from releasing the data, so an emphasis on SAT scores interacts with an emphasis on the most affluent students.

Decreasing Government Support

For so-called public institutions, the most important reason for rising prices is the withdrawal of government support. Historically, residents of a state paid taxes, and the state appropriated money to its higher education institutions. That money covered, or came close to covering, the cost of running the state's public colleges and universities. Students might pay something, but most of the college's money came from the state's appropriation.

If the orienting philosophy of neo-liberalism—the dominant approach of *both* parties since about 1980—is that "government is not the solution, government is the problem" and that cutting taxes is the solution to most of society's problems—then state appropriations should be (and have been) cut. If colleges and universities are getting less money from the government, then they have two choices: Let the quality of the education go down, or charge students more in tuition and fees, using money from students to make up for cuts in state appropriations. (A third choice, which we discuss in Chapter VI, and beloved by all administrators, is to "work smarter," "do more with less." This has usually meant cutting faculty and staff and hiring part-time employees.)

Once upon a time, states made it a priority to provide funding for public colleges and universities, and higher education budgets grew rapidly. That is no longer the case. From 1960–61 to 1970–71, the period of explosive growth in higher education, state expenditures almost quadrupled. In the next 20 years, from 1970–71 to 1990–91, state spending for higher education, in real terms, increased by 73.3 percent. Over the next 18 years, from 1990–91 to 2008–09, the increase was only 16.6 percent, and most of that came in the 1990s—the increase in this decade is only 3.7 percent (Center for the Study of Education Policy 2010).

What does that look like at the campus level? At UMass Amherst, the state appropriation in 2010 works out to $11,961 per undergraduate student. If this seems like a lot, it isn't. That is close to the national per pupil expenditure for each K-12 student ($11,052), with none of the buildings, labs, libraries, and other facilities that a college or university requires. Compared with a community college—say, Holyoke Community College, which receives only $1,853 per credit-earning student—the UMass Amherst amount seems like a lot.

The decline in state funding is reflected in the rapidly shrinking portion of public universities' budgets that comes from the state budget. Many public universities were once funded almost exclusively by state appropriation, just like many other aspects of government. No one pays an entrance fee for public schools; you don't pay to walk into a state park; you aren't charged for each book you take out of the public library; and you don't pay a fee to the fire department if your house is hit by lightning and catches fire. True, as part of the neo-liberal ideology, this notion of common shared services has begun to shift: "user fees" are being assessed for many functions traditionally paid for through the state budgets, which means through taxes.

Because public higher education has never been seen as a right—as kindergarten through high school has been for many decades—it has been at the forefront of the movement toward "self-funding." Each year the proportion of the total university budget provided by the state has declined. Some of the very biggest and most prestigious public universities have managed on a paltry percentage of their annual budget supplied by the state—Penn State now stands at 9.4 percent. This amount, however, includes everything Penn State does—including, for example, run dorms, food service, and a hospital. But even if we take out those items, state appropriations are only paying for 20.4 percent of a Penn State education, with tuition and fees covering 72.2 percent (Penn State 2010). A few flagship campuses have large endowments to draw on, as well as impressive networks of alumni. The University of Texas, for example, was given a huge endowment in the 1980s—the product of oil revenues rushing into the state's coffers. Its endowment stood at $12.1 billion in 2009. The University of Michigan's was over $6 billion (National Association of College and University Budget Officers 2010).

A few private universities also have large endowments. In Massachusetts, with its many old and wealthy institutions, there are nine institutions with endowments of a billion dollars or more. Harvard's stands around $36.9 billion. That endowment supports a medical school, law school, and numerous other operations, but if as a thought exercise we imagined that the endowment was exclusively for undergraduate students, that would work out to more than $5.5 million per student; at a 5 percent per year rate of return that would yield an annual income of $275,000 per student. (Remember that this is an unfair calculation, since much of the endowment supports the law school, medical school, and so on.)

And yet, even with these wealthy institutions—MIT, Wellesley, Brandeis, Williams, Amherst, Smith, Mt. Holyoke, Boston University—the median endowment of private colleges in the state is $32.1 million (Association of Independent Colleges and Universities in Massachusetts 2010: Slide 9). Most private colleges and universities rely on a combination of high tuition, annual gifts from alumni, and returns of their endowments.

If most private universities can't rely on endowments, that is ten times as true for (almost all) public universities, where endowments have not and could not replace state appropriations. The cuts in state appropriations have led to increased payments by students and parents. In 1980–81 states put 3.5 times as much money into public higher education as did parents and students; by 2006–07 states were only putting in 1.8 times as much as students and parents; recall that these figures include not just flagship universities, but also state and community colleges (National Center for Education Statistics 2010: Table 353 and 1995: Table 319). At the University of Massachusetts, in 2010, for the first time in our university's history, the total amount paid in tuition and fees by students and their parents exceeded the amount contributed by the state. One could argue that the University of Massachusetts has become a quasi-private university.

The easy—and partially correct—explanation for the cutback in state spending is that state budgets were in trouble. But as important as the total amount spent on higher education—which does fluctuate with the cycle of expansion and contraction of the economy—is the portion of state budgets that is spent on public higher education. Indeed, spending on higher education has not kept up with the overall increase in state revenues. States have had other priorities—prisons and health care expenditures. Since 1970 the number of people incarcerated in the United States has gone up more than sixfold, to a total of 2.4 million (U.S. Census Bureau 2009: Tables 335 and 337; 1972: Tables 261 and 266). States appropriate more per prisoner than they appropriate per (public) college student, with little resistance to constantly increasing the money spent on prisons. In Massachusetts, for example, in 1980 the state appropriated three times as much for higher education as it did for prisons; 25 years later the state was appropriating more for prisons than for higher education, a statement of the society's real priorities (Massachusetts Taxpayers Foundation 2003).

There were, of course, fiscal challenges that the states were not responsible for, especially the dramatic increase in health care expenditures. In the early 1980s the Reagan administration transferred the cost of Medicaid—health care for the poor—from the federal government to state governments. Federal appropriations to the states did not increase nearly as rapidly as health care costs, and states were left to make up the difference, putting a perpetual squeeze on state budgets. That squeeze will continue until the introduction of a single-payer health system—which at the moment looks to be a long way off.

It would be possible for both public and private institutions to try to respond to escalating tuition charges by increasing financial aid for the poor and working class. Exactly the opposite has happened. Colleges and universities have shifted from "needs based" aid—money given on the basis of the person's financial need, so larger payments go to lower-income students—to "merit-based" aid. So-called merit-based aid turns out to depend, to a great degree, on SAT scores and other indicators that give advantages to affluent students. At *public* universities, since the mid-1990s, the aid for "students from families of modest incomes, earning $20,000 to $39,999," went up by 21 percent—but students from families with incomes over $100,000 received 159 percent more. "At four-year private institutions, the story was similar, as aid to wealthy students surged 145 percent compared to just 15 percent for lower-income students" (Sacks 2007: 147; see also Folbre 2010). This means that as tuition and fees have skyrocketed, financial aid has made the problem worse, by shifting aid from those who need it most to those who need it less—although with tuition increasing so rapidly, even families with good incomes feel they need aid.

These policies—declining state support for higher education, rapidly increasing costs for students, shifting financial aid from needs based to merit based—are in practice promoted, or at the very least accepted as inevitable, by both political parties and by all major political actors. This book's authors both live in Massachusetts, where the legislature is 80 percent Democratic and the governor is a Democrat, who, when he came into office, promised "I will be a champion for public higher education." Nonetheless, the higher education budget gets cut, and tuition and fees get increased.

Because faculty, staff, and university officials make the best of a bad situation, the university continues to do its work and much of the impact is hidden from the public. In the next chapter, we show one of the most dramatic effects of declining funding and rising tuition—who gets to attend college.

DISCUSSION QUESTIONS

1. What tuition and fees are charged by your school? How much difference would it make in your life if tuition and fees were $2,401, the inflation-adjusted cost for public higher education in 1970–71? How much would it change the way people in general related to higher education today?

2. How much, if at all, do you work to help offset college costs? How much, if any, do you estimate you will owe when you graduate from college? In what ways do work and debt influence your college experience? How do they change the college experience for society more generally?

3. If you are at a public college or university, what has happened to its state funding over the last five or ten years? How do changes in state funding relate to student costs and the quality of education?

V: Who Goes?

❧

It is widely recognized that in many ways our society is highly unequal, and getting more so. Some people receive year-end bonuses of more than a million dollars; others work full-time all year long to earn $20,000. Some rent a place to live, drive an old, beat-up car, have no money in the bank, and owe thousands to the credit card companies; others have two (or three or four) homes, twice that many cars, many millions in their investment portfolios, and owe nothing on credit cards.

Those differences would seem to show that this is a highly unequal society, that the deck is stacked, and the game is crooked. The counter-argument, however, says:

> It's okay to have inequalities in wealth and income, because in our society everyone has a chance to make it to the top. Education is our great leveler, giving everyone, no matter what their family circumstances, a chance to improve their situation. Each generation has a chance to start anew.

Some version of this is central to the "American Dream," much celebrated by authors from Horatio Alger in the late nineteenth century, to James Truslow Adams who coined the term in the 1930s, to conservatives Edward Banfield and George Gilder in the 1970s and 1980s. Virtually everyone in the United States believes in this credo.

Suppose, for a minute, what is not at present the case: that every student attends an equally high-quality school. Even if all schools were the same, and all students had an equal chance to learn while at school, that would still not be enough to equalize education, much less to provide equal opportunity. Some kids would go home from school to a house filled with books and magazines and parents who could help them with their homework, and others would not; some would have easy access to computers and the Internet, others would not. The truth is that we have neither equal starting points—wealth, family situation, neighborhood resources—nor equal schools. However, we do maintain a commitment to universal, free, equal kindergarten through high school education.

The problem with our system of higher education is that three obstacles work in tandem: students come from different backgrounds, have unequal opportunities, and live in a nation that hasn't yet made a commitment to equal higher education. The odds are stacked high in favor of some and against others; in other words, the social structure makes it much easier for some than for others. An individual's effort clearly matters—sociologists refer to this as agency—but just how much difference does it make? It is clearly not the case that everything is determined by social structure, that if you are born poor you are certain to remain poor. And it is clearly not the case that everything depends on your own agency, that anyone who really tries will succeed, and anyone who has succeeded has done so on the basis of their own merits. The relative importance of structure and agency is one of the central debates in sociology.

Consider two families far apart on the education–income spectrum, and think about whether they are equally likely to attend college, and to graduate if they attend. Each family has three children ages 6 to 11, but they differ in significant ways. Family #1 is a two-parent family where both parents have bachelor's, master's and Ph.D. degrees from Ivy League institutions. Both have jobs as professors at a leading research university. The two parents' combined income of more than $150,000 puts the family into the top 10 percent of the population. The children have been taught from an early age that after high school comes college; they also know that their parents and grandparents have been setting money aside just for this purpose every year since their birth.

Family #2 also has three kids of about the same age, but in many ways is very different. The mother, call her Marisol, left an abusive relationship and with her kids went to a homeless shelter. Marisol graduated from high school but never attended college. While living in the homeless shelter, Marisol trained to become a Certified Nursing Assistant, and passed the test to do so. She was then hired by one of the most highly regarded nursing homes in the area—at a pay rate of $10 an hour, with a small differential on weekends, a differential eaten up by the taxi ride required to make it to work on time (since the bus on weekends arrives an hour after work begins). Marisol is lucky that her extended family is (usually) willing and able to provide childcare on weekends and for extra shifts.

The economics of the situation are challenging: without extra shifts, Marisol earns $17,264 a year. In addition Marisol and her children receive food stamps, limited childcare assistance, and some housing subsidy. Even with all that, money is *very* tight. Cable television, never mind a computer and Internet access, is out of the question.

If Marisol wanted to get ahead, the most plausible route for advancement would be to go to the local community college to be trained as a Licensed Practical Nurse. That would raise her pay to $22 an hour, but she would be lucky to complete the program in five years, assuming she could afford the expenses, get back and forth on public transportation, and find childcare for all the times she was in class.

Now consider the situation for these children as they reach college age. Neither Marisol nor any member of her family has attended, much less graduated from, college. Marisol lives in public housing in Springfield, a city that was recently in bankruptcy and has some of the lowest income areas in the state. Marisol doesn't know what an SAT test is, much less how to help her kids improve their scores, or how to choose among colleges, or dozens of other such things. It's certainly possible that her kids will go to college, and even graduate, but the odds are stacked against them, just as the odds are stacked in favor of Family #1's children.

How much difference does structural position make? If education was the "great leveler," Marisol's kids and Family #1's kids would be equally likely to attend college. But that is not what the data show us. Suppose we had 100 kids in Marisol's kids' situation (living in families in the bottom quarter of the income distribution, where neither parent had graduated from college). How many of those kids would graduate from college? On average, 9. Suppose we had another 100 kids, in Family #1's situation (in the top quarter of the income distribution, with at least one parent who had graduated from college). How many of those kids would graduate from college? On average, 68 (Bowen, Chingos, and McPherson 2009: 21). And if we were looking at families just like Family #1 above—with not just one parent a college graduate, but both graduates from Ivy League schools, not just in the top 25 percent of the income distribution but in the top 10 percent—then it would probably be 80 or 90 out of 100 kids graduating from college. Unless you believe that the kids in the Family #1's are seven times smarter and harder working, or seven times more deserving, than the kids in the Family #2's, the conclusion has to be that it is a lot harder to succeed if you start at the bottom.

Should colleges and universities be seeking out, and providing assistance to, the children of people like Family #1, or should schools be making extra efforts to open the doors to children like Marisol's? A very simplified story of the history of higher education in the United States suggests that for much of the first two centuries, the question wouldn't even have been asked—college was for the few and for the wealthy. For a brief few decades in the second half of the 20th century, there was both a firm commitment and real policies and resources dedicated to opening wider the doors to college. But with the rise of the neo-liberal ideology and the steady transformation of universities by business principles, the doors are swinging shut again. In the last 30 years, colleges and universities have increasingly shifted their emphasis from kids like Marisol's to those of affluent families (Sacks 2007: 152).

If you are a university-as-business administrator looking to make do with less funding from the state and to improve your *U.S. News* ranking, who would you recruit—the kids from affluent backgrounds with high SAT scores, or the kids from low-income families who struggled hard and show potential? The ranking system provides big rewards for higher SAT scores, and no rewards for increasing the number of students from disadvantaged backgrounds. And poorer kids only need more of a college's precious financial aid dollars. As a result, colleges are putting their money where their interests lie: they are increasingly likely to offer financial aid to Family #1 and deny it to Family #2.

Consider the number of students with Pell grants, the federal program to provide assistance to low-income students. So-called top colleges and universities—that is, those whose students have the highest SAT scores—have very few Pell grant students.

Harvard and Princeton, for example, were two of the three schools with the lowest percentage of students having Pell grants. It is still the public universities that educate students with the greatest financial need. Our university, UMass Amherst, for example, has more Pell Grant recipients than Amherst College, Boston College, Harvard, MIT, Smith, Tufts, and Wellesley—combined. But public universities as well are trying to be upwardly mobile. The University of Michigan and the University of Wisconsin substantially increased their average SAT scores in the 1990s and early 2000s—at the same time as they substantially cut the number of Pell grant recipients (in Michigan's case to half what it had been) (Sacks 2007: 159–62). That is, Michigan and Wisconsin became "better" schools—by keeping out the low-income students a public university is designed to serve. (Interestingly, Michigan pushed out its low-income students at exactly the same time that it fought hard in the courts for its right to make extra efforts to recruit students of color.)

As public support for colleges is reduced (see Chapter IV), as tuition and fees skyrocket, and as financial aid is shifted away from poor and working-class students to students with affluent backgrounds and high SAT scores, students are going into greater and greater debt in order to go to college at all. These days, two out of three students getting a bachelor's degree have student debt. At public universities "only" 62 percent of graduates are in debt, at private non-profit universities 72 percent are, and at private for-profit universities 96 percent are. For those graduating with debt, the average level of debt was $23,200 in 2008. (Compare this to our discussion in the last chapter: students could easily graduate with zero debt in 1971.) Obviously, in any such situation some students are graduating with lower debts, and some graduate with much higher debts (Project on Student Debt 2010). In the 2007–08 year, 206,000 students graduated from college with more than $40,000 in loan debt, nine times the number who graduated with this level of debt in 1996. Those high-debt students represented about 10 percent of all graduates that year (College Board 2009; Lieber 2010; Project on Student Debt 2010). The need to pay off debt limits the kinds of jobs that some students can take; one report concluded that more than one out of every three public four-year college graduates would face financial hardships if they worked as a social worker when they had to repay their student loan debt (Swarthout 2006).

And those are the ones who graduate. An increasing problem is that students are accumulating large amounts of debt and not even graduating. One major culprit is the for-profit and online universities, who make it exceptionally easy to register and take out loans, and exceptionally hard to complete classes and degrees. This is no accident, as high rates improve the bottom line: when students drop out the university keeps the money but has fewer expenses because they now have fewer students. This is also a problem for students at public and private non-profit colleges and universities. As costs rise, debt rises. Strapped colleges don't offer enough required courses, leading students to need extra years to graduate, expanding their debt, pushing them to take on more work, and leading many to drop out. It is a dangerous cycle of easy debt leading to default that is eerily like the mortgage default crisis that brought the economy to its knees in 2008 (Marklein 2009). Our colleges and universities are graduating—or not graduating—a growing class of people who will be burdened by debt for years if not decades.

Sociologists these days often talk about the role of race, class, and gender in shaping one's life chances and experience. For many issues, gender and race are crucial, and probably explain more of the inequality than does class. That is not the case for access to higher education. In the last generation colleges and universities have taken big strides in advancing gender and to a lesser extent race equality. But class inequalities have increased. In 1966, there were three men in college for every two women; today, the situation is almost reversed, with women more than 57 percent of all college students. That is, women have gone from being underrepresented to being overrepresented (National Center for Education Statistics 2010: Table 189). In 1976 black students were 9.4 percent of college students (compared to 11.6 percent of the total population), and Latino students were 3.5 percent of college students (compared with 5.3 percent of the population). Today, black students are 13.5 percent of college students (compared with 13.7 percent of the population), and Latinos are 11.9 percent of college students (compared with 15.4 percent of the population) (National Center for Education Statistics 2010: Table 227; U.S. Census Bureau 2009: Table 6; U.S. Census Bureau 1977: Tables 16 and 34).

We don't have the same positive statistics for class. The university-as-business model has clear implications for social class and college attendance, and the results are evident in the statistics. Over the last 40 years the number of people earning a bachelor's degree has increased. But for whom has it increased? The answer is that *all* of the increase in people graduating from college has come from people in the top half of the income distribution. The bottom quarter of the population, indeed the bottom half, is no more likely to get a college degree today than they were in 1970—but people in the top half of the income distribution are substantially more likely to graduate from college (Sacks 2007: 118). This means that college attendance is becoming more unequal by class. One study showed that the college admissions process at elite schools gave admissions advantages to athletes, students of color, and the children of alumni, but none to students from low-income families—in fact, they were subject to a small disadvantage as compared with others with similar grades and scores (Bowen and Bok 2000; Sacks 2007: 166).

The argument might be made that the increased inequality in who attends college and graduates from it is not really about colleges at all, it is about the inequalities in grade school and high school and the fact that some people receive better educations and are more qualified for college. Even if they are bright and hard-working, kids like Marisol's simply do not get as good an education as the kids in Family #1, so they have lower test scores, are less likely to be admitted to college, and don't do as well if they get to college. This may show that there are inequalities in our society, it could be claimed, but does not show that there are inequalities for which the colleges themselves are responsible.

It *is* true that it is harder for kids like Marisol's to get high test scores, but let's consider what happens when they are able to do so. To put it in the starkest terms: smart poor kids are no more likely to attend college than dumb rich kids. Less memorably, but with greater precision: people from the bottom 25 percent of the socio-economic scale, who have achievement test scores in the top quarter of the distribution, have a 78 percent chance of being in college two years after they graduate from high school. At the other end, people from the top 25 percent of the socio-economic scale, whose achievement test scores put them in the bottom quarter of the distribution, have a 77 percent chance of being in college two years later (Lee 1999: 15).

And it's not just a question of who makes it to college, but also of who graduates. Consider, for example, students who go to ordinary state system universities (that is, not the flagship public university). How likely is someone to graduate in four years? If the student comes from the bottom half of the income distribution, and neither of their parents had a college degree, then the chances are only 32 out of 100 that they will graduate in four years (and only 55 in 100 that they will do so by the end of their sixth year). If the student comes from the top half of the income distribution, and has at least one parent with a college degree, their chances of graduating in four years goes up to 52 out of 100 (and their chances of graduating by the end of the their sixth year go up to 74 out of 100) (Bowen, Chingos and McPherson 2009: 37).

The inequality in who makes it to college, and who graduates once they enter, means that many people are denied the opportunity to open their minds and explore new ideas. It also means that they earn less than they would have, and are denied the opportunities that income makes available. From the perspective of the broader economy, this inequality means we have vast amounts of underdeveloped human capital and, very directly, lost tax revenue and economic activity by businesses that need these workers' skills and creativity.

Colleges and universities aren't just victims of the larger society; their own actions, driven by the university-as-business model, help create the inequality. A full solution, however, would require policies that address not only the problems in higher education, but also the larger inequalities in our society.

A first step would be to address the condition of workers in colleges and universities, which has steadily declined over the past generation, and is the subject of the next chapter.

DISCUSSION QUESTIONS

1. How easy (or difficult) would it be for the children of Family #1 to graduate from college? For Marisol's kids to do so? What do the statistics indicate?

2. Imagine you were a university president, trying to improve your school, and knowing you would be fired if you couldn't show results within three years. What sorts of students, from what backgrounds, would you try to recruit, and why? What opposition, and what support, would you be likely to encounter?

3. A high school student's record of achievement makes a difference in their odds of attending college, but so does their family income and whether one or more of their parents has graduated from college. What is the relative impact of these different factors?

4. For those students who do make it to college, does a student's family income and parents' education have an impact on their chances of graduating from college? Put your sociological imagination to work to make informed guesses about the reasons for this.

VI: Who Works?

❧━◦━❧

W ho works at our colleges or universities?

The question may seem of secondary importance to the future of higher education, but we want to argue it is not. First, 3.6 million people work at colleges and universities, making them an important part of our economy. Second, the conditions under which people work have a substantial impact on the experience of higher education for students, and on the quality of the research and teaching that are done there. Finally, colleges and universities were in so many ways constructed to be different than the rest of society—in how they are governed, what they reward, the pace of activity, the openness to the widest range of free expression. So, how different are colleges and universities from other organizations in how they treat the people who do the work?

One fact to start this discussion: just 30 years ago, the average student had a better than 50 percent chance to walk into a classroom and find at the head of the class a tenured or tenure-track faculty member, evaluated by his or her peers, and with a long-term commitment to the college or university. In 2010, the chance was about one in three. More likely, the teacher would be a committed but vastly overworked and underpaid adjunct faculty member, hired year to year, without the kinds of credentials and support of those in the tenure system, who are hired for a six-year period with the possibility of lifetime employment. We suggest that this transformation has large and dire consequences for higher education.

Over the last three decades colleges and universities have been **Wal-Marted**, a process very much associated with the university-as-business model, and our society's general turn to neo-liberalism. The push has been made to move away from full-time workers—whether they be faculty, or a raft of other workers like janitors, food servers, clerical staff, and assorted professionals—with good pay and benefits to part-time workers with low pay and no benefits. Often this is accomplished through contracting out the work; in the case of faculty, the college itself employs the part-time, low-paid, no-benefits teachers. One difference from Wal-Mart, however, is that Wal-Mart boasts of its low prices, but the Wal-Marting of the university has happened at exactly the time that prices (tuition and fees) have risen most rapidly. In this chapter, we focus on what has happened to faculty, but many of the same issues apply to food service, or buildings and grounds, and virtually every other type of work at colleges and universities.

If we go back to the faculty governance model, the ideal figure and the center of attention was (and still is) the long-term faculty member, dedicated to the institution. Such an ideal person is not primarily focused on money or personal advancement, but rather on the pursuit of knowledge and truth, whatever the obstacles, and on teaching and mentoring students. Taking a stand on principle is the highest good, the respect of your colleagues the greatest reward, the long-term interests of the institution a guiding principle. What should be celebrated is not a particular individual, but the faculty as a whole; the noteworthy professor does not rule over others but rather is a kind of first-among-equals. The admired administrator is not the CEO who boosted donations, but the long-time faculty member promoted to dean or provost who brings his or her commitments to teaching and research to the role of administrator, in effect being an advocate for the faculty, not their boss.

In the university-as-business model, the central figure is the CEO administrator, who comes in from the outside, shakes things up, increases fundraising, raises the school's ranking, and then moves on to a more prestigious university to do the same all over again. Although the school's CEO is the most obvious such hero, the same attitude can apply to the admissions officer who attracts the highest-scoring students, likely from out of state, or the "development officer" who raises alumni donations. The administrator looking to build their career needs to introduce some signature initiatives that will show measurable results within the next three or four years, and thus form the basis for the administrator's jump to the next university.

To accomplish that, the administrator needs to put together a "team" of subordinate administrators, whose loyalty and future promotion depend on the success of the administrator (as opposed to the success of the institution). For that to work, the administrator feels the need to hire a new set of administrators from the outside, or to reorganize the institution so that some people can be promoted, and those promoted can owe their positions—and their loyalty—to the new administrator. (Typically no one is actually demoted, which would create enemies; since no one is demoted, but many are promoted, the ranks of the administration—managers but also support personnel—swell.) Over the past two decades, the number of administrative support personnel has far outpaced the growth in student enrollment and the teachers that instruct them, nearly doubling from 1987 to 2007: "The shift means that the core academic operations, teaching and research, are now a smaller piece of the pie" (Brainard, Fain, and Masterson 2009).

For the university-as-business model, subordinate administrators, and non-teaching professionals, have another important advantage over faculty. Tenured faculty have a great deal of independence; it is difficult (although by no means impossible) to coerce them. Administrators and non-teaching professionals, however, are much easier to fire or reassign. For these administrators, and for the university-as-business model, one of the biggest problems with reorienting the university to the business model is the faculty and, more specifically, the tenured faculty. Indeed, tenure itself is for the entrepreneurial administrator a nightmare, for tenure creates a unique class of workers at the institution who have the job security to say no, to refuse to go along, and worse yet, to speak out publicly against the actions of administrators. (To be fair, there are many administrations who honestly say they are committed to the idea of tenure but insist that their hands are tied—there is not enough money, so they need to hire cheap teaching labor.)

In the view of administrators, business executives, and trustees, this is perhaps the most compelling argument against tenure: "The tenure system is inflexible and limits administrators' ability to improve schools and departments" (Immerwahr 1999), according to 83 percent of the business executives surveyed. Trustees believe that tenure creates "an unacceptably potent buffer against centralized initiatives ... . Tenure weakens the relative authority of executives" (Chait 2002: 15). It is no accident that one of the prime targets of administrators in the new university-as-business model is tenure.

Direct assaults on the idea of tenure have been attempted but until very recently with little impact. Rather, administrators have achieved the same goal by replacing retiring tenure-system faculty—who are full-time, well-paid, benefited, independent-minded, and able to resist administrative pressure—with part-time and adjunct faculty, who don't get benefits, are paid a fraction as much as tenure-system faculty, and can easily be replaced if they speak out against the administration. It seems that for some administrators, the ideal is that each department should have one full-time faculty member to serve as department chair, and all the other faculty should be part-time adjuncts. In this regard, college "CEOs" are not that different from private-sector CEOs, who also look to replace full-time, fully-benefited, decently paid employees whenever possible, sending their jobs to China if feasible, and if not having the work done in the United States by undocumented immigrants who (the CEOs hope) won't have the leverage to change things if their rights are violated. Indeed, the analogy is becoming increasingly direct: as universities move toward more online education (in part because the market will bear similar tuition rates, but universities can hire adjunct teachers to do the work), they are looking well beyond their own community, or even the nation, for low-paid teachers.

For those who remain on the tenure track, salaries have, as we discussed in Chapter IV, remained stagnant while health insurance and other costs have gone steadily up. Tenure was both a central protection for free speech among faculty and, frankly, a way of recruiting highly accomplished individuals (some of the most educated people in a nation) to forego higher-paid work in exchange for a large measure of job security (Clawson 2009). As we look 10 or 20 years into the future, the position of professor will look increasingly less attractive as a career, which can only diminish the quality of teaching and research that will take place there.

The neo-liberal ideology has been remarkably successful in transforming the nature of university teaching in just a generation. As recently as 1980, when Ronald Reagan was elected president, tenure-system faculty—that is, full-time assistant, associate, and full professors—were 55 or 56 percent of all faculty. According to recent government data, tenure-system faculty were only 31 percent of all faculty in 2007 (National Center for Education Statistics various years). The shift to non-tenure-system faculty has taken place in both private and public institutions and at all levels from research universities to community colleges.

The most pernicious part of this is a rise in part-time faculty, especially at lower-ranking institutions. They have gone from 22 percent of all faculty in 1970 to 43 percent in 2003. Part-time faculty are most prevalent at community colleges (67 percent of all faculty) and least significant at public doctoral institutions (22 percent). At doctoral institutions, the move away from tenure has not, for the most part, meant the rise of part-time faculty, but rather the rise of full-time non-tenure-track faculty. That form of the move away from tenure is not as destructive to the teaching mission of the institution—such faculty at least have offices, teach multiple courses, and are more likely to stay from year to year so students can find them later—but it is deadly for the research mission of the university. Since the movement to full-time non-tenure-track faculty is concentrated at research universities, it means that exactly the places that should be leading our nation's cutting-edge research are having researchers replaced with people who may be excellent teachers, but who (for the most part) do not have impressive records of research. To what extent is this shift being made? In the fall of 2003, for full-time instructional faculty at doctoral institutions, among newer faculty, 32.8 percent of the male faculty hired, and 47.7 percent of the female faculty, were not on the tenure track (National Center for Education Statistics 2004: Table 8). These numbers underestimate the problem because they don't reflect the fact that most part-time faculty have a much higher teaching responsibility. While a tenured faculty member who is committed to a research lab advises a dozen graduate students, and serves on several university committees, teaches only four courses a year, a non-tenure-track faculty member might very well teach eight courses. In addition, graduate student teachers are teaching a growing number of courses at universities. So, in fact, the total percentage of courses and students taught by graduate, adjunct, or full-time, non-tenure-track faculty is higher than the ratios above suggest.

Students might reasonably ask: Well, if these people are good teachers (Cross and Goldenberg 2009), and maybe even are hired for several years in a row (which is as long as a student is in school), why should it matter if tenure-track faculty are being replaced with adjunct and non-tenure-track faculty? It makes a difference for at least two reasons. First, and most immediately significant to students: tenure-track faculty are likely to be leading figures in their field, scholars recognized for their contributions. That is almost never true of non-tenure-track faculty. One of the foundational arguments for research universities, where faculty conduct high-level research and also teach 18-year-old students, is the belief that students will learn more—about the subject and the pursuit of knowledge—from faculty who are working at the cutting edge of their fields. If the only concern is good teaching about the currently accepted research, that may be as likely to be found at community colleges as at universities. But there is an important benefit for students to learn from people with a significant record of their own scholarship.

A second reason that it matters whether universities use tenure-system faculty, or switch to vulnerable non-tenure-system faculty, is that if there is to be a serious effort to reverse the direction of higher education today—from the university-as-business, raise costs, and soak the students model, to something else (see Chapter VII)—then it will be important that faculty be part of that effort. The faculty with a life-time commitment to one institution develop a long-range vision of the university, and (sometimes) a willingness to stand up for that vision, even against their own administrators. A not incidental side-effect of the decline of tenure-track faculty is the decline in the size of the group that can speak for a different ideal of higher education.

To get a sense of the difference between tenure-system and non-tenure-system faculty, consider what happens when the sociology department at the University of Massachusetts Amherst does a job search. If the search is for a tenure-track position, then as a nationally ranked department at a good university, the position is nationally advertised and the search attracts 250 or more applications. A committee of five tenure-system faculty and two graduate students reviews all applications and chooses four people to come to campus for interviews. Those four people come to campus for two-day interviews, with each presenting a public talk, meeting with faculty individually, and meeting with students. Faculty read the written work of the four finalists, check references, and vigorously debate who will contribute most to the university and department.

If the search is for a non-tenure-system faculty member, the position is locally advertised, the search attracts a half-dozen to a dozen applicants, and the department chair makes the choice, possibly without meeting any of the candidates, and frequently without consulting other faculty. The tenure-system faculty member represents a long-term commitment to the future of the department and the university, a decision collectively made by all faculty; the non-tenure-system faculty member is (at least seen as) a short-term stop-gap, and is a decision made by a single person. (Sometimes that non-tenure-system person ends up staying for years, and sometimes the person ends up being excellent; every effort is of course made to hire the best person the department chair can identify.) A massive effort wouldn't make sense for a one-year position, and often these positions are in any case being filled at the last minute (as opposed to the tenure-system hires, which take place nine months before the person will begin work).

Whether a department hires a tenure-system or a non-tenure-system faculty member, the aim is to get someone who is a good teacher. Because the non-tenure-system faculty member is being hired only for teaching, despite a limited search it is often possible to come up with a talented teacher; if the person doesn't work out the hope is that they will not be rehired. The tenure-system faculty member is the product of a much more competitive search, but their research potential is likely to be the most important factor in the decision to hire them. Some administrators and experts are arguing that universities should move to a two-tier faculty, with a handful of highly paid research stars who rarely meet a student, surrounded by dozens of part-time faculty paid not much more than minimum wage to do the actual teaching.

Universities are moving in this direction, whether or not that is seen as the official goal. The key decisions are not being made by faculty, however, but rather by "CEO" administrators, who have consistently moved to replace well-paying long-term jobs with poorly paid short-term jobs, most notably for faculty but for a range of other workers as well. For those who argue that this shift is supposed to be good for colleges and universities, the problem is to explain why the more elite the institution, the more it has continued to rely on tenure-system faculty (who remain dominant in, say, the Ivy League), and the lower-ranking the college, the more it relies on part-time faculty (as is true, for example, at community colleges). They must also explain why the public university system of the decades after World War II was built almost exclusively around tenure-track faculty who managed to create the most admired higher education system in the world, producing the most college graduates in the world, who anchored American prosperity for a generation. And finally, for those who argue that the move to vulnerable part-time faculty will save money, the challenge is to explain why this shift has taken place at exactly the same time that costs have sky-rocketed.

This move to a more disposable faculty is very much a part of the university-as-business model, which sees top administrators as the most valuable part of the university, and the people who most deserve to be rewarded. It should be no surprise that administrator pay has gone up more than faculty pay—even full-time faculty pay—every year for more than a decade (American Association of University Professors 2010; Strout 2006; López-Rivera 2010). All of this begs the question of priorities: if money is scarce, which is more important—hiring two more tenure-track faculty, to enable each senior to take a 15-student senior seminar, or putting the same money into hiring one Chief Assistant to the Assistant Chief of the Branding Initiative, to assist in coming up with a new slogan for the university? Administrators routinely proclaim their commitment to students, faculty, and teaching; in practice, however, they almost always choose to put their money into the Chief Assistant to the Assistant Chief, because—in the eyes of the administrator—a new university slogan is more important.

In a way, the question of who works at our colleges and universities, which we suggested might seem like a lower-priority question, touches on some of the most central questions of public higher education: what do we care most about, teachers or administrators, the model of an independent-minded teaching scholar or an overworked teacher? What is the goal of a university, the delivery of credit hours in as cheap a manner as possible, or the creation of a thinking community dedicated to the pursuit and communication of knowledge?

DISCUSSION QUESTIONS

1. Do you know which of the instructors for your courses are tenured, untenured but in the tenure system, and not in the tenure system (on contracts, part-time, graduate students, and so on)?

2. If faculty are good teachers, does it matter if they are not recognized scholars hired through a national search and with national reputations? In what ways, if at all, does it matter? If you were choosing a college, and knew that the faculty at two schools were equally good teachers, but at only one were the faculty leading scholars, how much would that matter to you?

3. If administrators move to hire more part-time and temporary faculty, at dramatically lower wages and without benefits, what effects is this likely to have on colleges and universities over the long term?

4. For at least the last decade, each year administrator pay has increased more than faculty pay. Is that similar to, or different from, what is happening in the larger society? If this continues for the next decade and beyond, what are the likely consequences?

VII: Choosing a Future

In 1962, Thomas Kuhn wrote *The Structure of Scientific Revolutions*, a book about how science changes. He argued that scientific ideas become so entrenched, accepted almost as natural law, that it is impossible to slowly move science in a new direction. Rather, a thoroughly accepted idea can only be overturned in what he termed a "paradigm shift."

We live now within a neo-liberal paradigm, with its celebration of markets, distrust of government, and hatred of taxes accepted as the starting point for all political debates. Proposals that reject this paradigm are seen as out beyond the edge of reason. There is a nationwide—and international—set of ideas, which we have discussed throughout this book, that circulate as part of the neo-liberal ideology, and they find their ways into the workings of large corporations and small, big cities and small towns, public and private universities.

For the future of higher education in the United States to be strong, we will need a paradigm shift, where what is now at the center moves to the periphery, and we bring the periphery to the center.

The Dominant Vision

But, first, the center. By way of summary of the previous chapters, let's consider the system of higher education that is being implemented by those who are setting the course for today's colleges and universities.

- Because the public sector is being starved, we must increasingly rely on the private sector, and especially on for-profit higher education. Funding for public higher education will continue to be reduced, and government resources (such as Pell grants) will flow to the growing for-profit universities.

- Funding for colleges and universities will come from students and their parents. People may grumble about the costs, and may suffer hardships to attend, but there is a plentiful supply of families who can and will pay. Public universities have the market position to charge higher prices, and will do so, thus saving money for the taxpayers and helping to avoid tax increases.

- The goal of colleges and universities will continue to be bringing in more revenue (through tuition, research grants, and increased endowments) and raising the average SAT scores of those attending in order to improve the school's ranking in *U.S. News*. Schools will be sold to students as ways to raise their lifetime earnings, and to the (business) community as providing the research needed for economic growth.

- In order to carry out this program, the university needs to be run more like a business. Colleges and universities need highly paid CEOs who know how to market a product, generate revenue, and balance a budget. Faculty governance gets in the way of this, and will be reduced as much as possible. Obviously students shouldn't have a say in shaping the university, except insofar as they "vote" with their tuition dollars.

- Higher education will increasingly be for the children of the affluent. But this is not something to lament, some scholars and policy makers are arguing. Perhaps the poor and working class don't really belong in college anyway—their education hasn't properly prepared them for college, they don't have the money to afford it, and therefore they will be likely to drop out. They would be better off saving their money and not starting college in the first place (Malanga 2008).

- Less funding, more focus on private funds, and responding to the market also mean that colleges and universities will continue to replace the professor committed to a college for a lifetime, who was both a noted scholar and a classroom teacher, who received good pay and benefits and had a say in shaping the curriculum and running the college, with a few well-paid stars (who don't teach, or rarely teach) and lots of low-paid, part-time faculty who have no job security and are highly vulnerable if they try to speak up about what they see as best for students and the university.

We Can Go Another Way

We reject this neo-liberal ideology and offer an alternative. Much of what we suggest would be recognizable to leading policy makers and educational leaders a couple of decades ago, and might again seem obvious within a couple of decades.

We begin with two propositions, one positive and one negative.

First, we believe what most economists accept: the best long-term investment for any society is education. One economist at the University of California at Davis has analyzed dozens of countries over two centuries and found a remarkable correlation between level of investment in education and economic growth (Lindert 2004). It has been estimated that the long-term return on common stocks is 6.3 percent. The return to a society in terms of increased taxes due to greater education among a nation's people is 13.3 percent. Other nations, especially rapidly growing ones, understand this, which is why they are investing heavily in their university systems, using the United States in the 1950s and 1960s as the model. As a result, the United States no longer leads the world in percentage of college graduates in the general population; indeed we are tenth, and the only nation of those ten where older adults have more education than younger adults (National Center for Higher Education Management Systems 2007). In the midst of the debate over stimulus funds to help ease the recession, Michael Porter, a Harvard Business School professor, said the same thing. He has argued for more stimulus dollars to support public higher education, because his research shows it is the most valuable type of infrastructure this country can build (Brooks 2008). Businesses, as well, understand the importance of education, which is why they routinely report that the single most important factor in decisions about where to locate is the level and quality of education of the workforce (Cohen 2000; Ady 1997).

Second, we simply reject the starting point for most political discussions: There is no money. If ever there were a time when there was no money, it was the Great Depression of the 1930s, when one out of three people was unemployed, wages dropped drastically for those employed, the stock market tanked, and businesses and banks went bankrupt. And yet the 1930s is the time when the United States introduced Social Security, unemployment compensation, federally guaranteed mortgages, government protection for workers forming unions, and a wide range of other progressive policies. The money is always available, if the decisionmakers regard the issue as a real priority.

Rejecting the no-money premise may seem shocking, as virtually every day for the past two decades there have been declarations that there is simply not enough money. We agree that at present there is no money in public coffers to pay for public colleges and universities (and for roads, and libraries, and health care for the poor, and many other things a civilization commonly pays for together, through taxes). But that is due not to the lack of money.

The story of the past three decades is the story of the transfer of wealth from the pockets of the lower and middle classes to the pockets of the wealthy. Americans are more productive—that is, they produce more products and services per person—than ever before, and yet wages for the vast majority of people have remained stagnant (Mishel, Bernstein, and Shierholz 2009). The explanation is that money is being funneled northward, to the wealthiest people in the nation. It is a simple equation: a person picks more apples in a day than ever before (or cares for more patients, or teaches more students), but the employer pays them the same amount and pockets the extra profit.

And even as wealth has flowed upward, taxes have flowed downward. The wealthy have seen their incomes skyrocket but, ironically or perversely, have reduced the share of their wealth that they contribute to our common life. So, the starting point for our proposals is an insistence on reversing the current policy of fattening the wealthy and starving the general public.

We believe in free higher education, life-long learning, democracy on campus and not just in a November voting booth, colleges and universities that model the sorts of practices we would like to see for society as a whole (for jobs, the environment, and much more), and an education that is not *only* about "increasing your earning potential" or "boosting economic growth."

The University as a Model Democratic Institution

Throughout this book we have shown the consequences of the university-as-business model. We believe in a long-standing, democratic alternative which was at the heart of the protest movements of the 1960s and thereafter.

While the faculty governance model is much preferable to the university-as-business model and is based on a notion of democracy, it is a limited notion: If it is based on workers' control, it is control only by the most privileged set of workers, the faculty. Although faculty governance can protect basic values and stand up to outside attacks, faculty governance can also become insular and self-interested.

We believe that students as well should have a substantial role in shaping the institution, by having real authority on boards of trustees and in student governments. Similarly, the groups virtually ignored in most discussions of higher education—non-faculty staff, such as clerical workers, maintenance staff, and non-teaching professionals who make up the majority of workers on any college or university campus—deserve a real voice in running the university. In many cases, it is the staff who spend the most time with students on a daily basis. Finally, we believe that if the university is to serve the larger society, then there should be an established place for members of the broader community. The community could be involved not just in shaping the teaching mission of the college, but also by indicating the kinds of research that are most needed to address ordinary people's problems. We need, in essence, a renewed but democratically updated commitment to the land-grant mission that led to the founding of most of our finest public research universities—a commitment to scholarship and teaching in the service of the state and nation.

There is a direct connection between the rise of the university-as-business model and the declining political support for higher education, especially public higher education. When students are treated like customers (and come to see themselves that way), and faculty and staff are mere employees, as opposed to active members in a community of educators and scholars—that is a formula for weakening loyalty and dedication to an institution and the very idea of higher education. We believe that a democratic model of higher education is not only right and fair, but builds a broad support for the unique mission of higher education.

At a very basic level, we believe that a college or university should be an ideal place, not a typical one—an ideal workplace (where workers are treated as we would wish to be treated, not as a business executive would like them to be treated); a place of maximum free expression; a pioneer in sustainable design and energy efficiency. We need to recover and enhance the idea that the university doesn't just house laboratories, but is itself is a laboratory.

One of the most common metaphors about a university is that it is an "ivory tower," somehow removed from society. We imagine quite the opposite: a place that draws in the fullness of a society's people and challenges, and reflects back to it models to emulate.

But our system of higher education can only be this model if there is a dramatic reinvestment in the university's mission. This will happen not through a small increase in Pell grants to low-income students, or a 2 percent increase in state funding for state colleges and universities. It requires something much more radical, which would infuse colleges and universities with a massive amount of new funds but would also send a message of commitment that would have endless ripple effects.

We are speaking, of course, of free higher education.

Free Higher Education

Imagine that public higher education was literally a birthright of every resident. And then stories like this would not have to be invented by us:–

- Marisol's (the nursing assistant we discussed in Chapter II) daughter—someone highly unlikely to attend college in 2010—attends the University of Massachusetts because it is now tuition free. Unburdened by fear of debt, she chooses to be an art major. Because she only needs to contribute to her room and board costs, she works just a few hours a week and therefore manages to graduate in four years. She becomes an art teacher in a Massachusetts public school and by the age of 22 starts to earn a living, save for a house and retirement, and pay taxes. Like the majority who are college-educated, she doesn't smoke, is active in community affairs, and has the background to raise her (eventual) children to perform well in school and themselves become good, educated citizens.

- A young man graduates from high school and heads to work in an Alabama Toyota plant. He works there for a decade before the plant shuts down and the work is shipped off to Mexico. He heads to the local university to answer a major need in the aging nation: nursing.

- A young mother works full-time but chooses to take online courses offered by the community college located 40 miles away and then participate in an intensive on-campus course, for a week every summer. By the time her young children are in school full-time, she has earned her degree in accounting.

- The lucky high school graduate who found a job working in a local company and spent 25 years there retires and decides to finally get his college degree that he long wished he had gotten. This late bloomer becomes an important novelist and enriches the lives of millions.

Given the rhetoric about the importance, for individual and nation, of higher education, one would think we were not far from making these stories reality. Indeed, it seems that everyone agrees that a college education is necessary for success. A high school degree just won't do it, say President Obama and President Bush's Secretary of Education. The sentiment is bipartisan, and so has been the failure.

The more important higher education has become to a person's chances of success and to our society's chances to compete globally, the harder we have made it for students and their families to afford a college education. Thirty years ago, state and local governments put in $3.99 for every dollar that students and parents paid; today states put in $1.76 for every dollar, less than half what they contributed a generation ago (Clawson 2009). The result: millions of students have left college with massive debt that has limited their life chances. Millions more are simply unable to afford higher education. This isn't just a tragedy for the individual but for society.

Our society has a peculiar arrangement that is not just accepted, but largely unquestioned. For a high school student attending twelfth grade in a public school, education is free. But when the student moves to thirteenth grade in a public school—that is, becomes a freshman at, say, the University of Massachusetts Amherst—education is no longer free; in fact, tuition and fees (for an in-state student) are currently $11,732. Why should the twelfth grade of public education be free but the thirteenth grade cost thousands of dollars?

In the 17th century the first Marquess of Halifax wrote that "A man that should call everything by its right name would hardly pass the streets without being knocked down as a common enemy" (Herman 1982: 1). The right name for our society's current policy of charging thousands of dollars for *public* higher education is "outrageous" and perhaps "irrational." And yet we live in a world where to suggest that public higher education should be free is regarded as lunacy.

It was in our home state of Massachusetts that Horace Mann declared and then convinced the state that elementary education should be universal and paid for by the public. Later, we—all of us, via the imperfect mechanisms of democratic government—decided that a basic education meant high school. We are now in a transitional place, where we understand college to be as essential to success as high school was understood to be in the middle of the last century, and yet we charge citizens thousands of dollars to get a college education.

Many people agree that higher education should be free, but respond: "How could we afford it?" The cost for the federal government to pay all the tuition and fees paid by all students, at all public higher education institutions, would have been $44.8 billion in the 2006–07 academic year (National Center for Education Statistics 2010: Table 352), the most recent year for which the data have been reported.

More than $45 billion a year would of course be needed to provide free public higher education. The minor reason is that tuition and fees have gone up significantly since 2006–07. The more important reason is that if public colleges and universities were free, suddenly many more people would go to school—which is part of the point. The increased students would add to costs, but costs would still be manageable; maybe costs would go to $100 billion a year. Such a program would be politically popular, would once again make America the unequivocal leader in higher education, would boost economic growth, and would lead to an explosion of learning.

Forty-five (or one hundred) billion dollars a year is not a trivial expense, but it is far less than the cost of the Bush-era tax breaks for the top 5 percent of the population ($1.3 trillion), or the Iraq and Afghanistan wars ($1 trillion), or the bank bailout (a minimum of $800 billion). Consider just one of the many possible sources of funding. Right now, a large majority of the population have to pay Social Security taxes on all of their wage income. High wage earners, however, don't have to do so. They pay Social Security taxes on the first $106,000 a year of their income, but then stop paying for the rest of the year. (For some, that $106,000 threshold comes early in January.) Suppose high wage earners had to do what the rest of us do, and pay Social Security taxes on all of their wages. How much extra revenue what that generate? It would bring in an extra $115 billion a year (Acuff and Levins 2010: 24), more than enough to fund free public higher education.

But why give everyone free higher education? Wouldn't it make more sense to concentrate the aid on those who need it more? This is the argument for a "high tuition–high aid" model, where the wealthy supposedly pay full fare and those on the lower end of the scale supposedly get financial aid. This is the system we operate under now, and it has produced the inequalities and lack of access we have discussed in this book. The reasons are many: high tuition scares off lower-income students; much of financial aid is in the form of loans, which saddles students with huge debts on graduating. And, anyway, the "high aid" has increasingly gone to middle and even upper-middle-class students, as we discussed in Chapter V.

But we reject this view because of what history shows us: social programs that are needs-based are always seen as a form of charity, and suffer repeated cut-backs. "High tuition and high aid" almost always becomes "High tuition and reduced aid." In Massachusetts, the state's primary financial aid program for low-income students, Mass Grant, has been cut in half over the past decade, even as tuition and fees have more than doubled. On the other hand, programs that are universal, available to everyone, come to be accepted as totally legitimate, as entitlements that can't be touched. Consider Social Security and Medicare, our nation's two most important entitlement programs—both of which, significantly, apply to older people, with no equivalent programs for younger people. In the summer of 2009, a grassroots, conservative movement erupted on the political scene. The "Tea Party" rallied around the country against "government health care," even as a number of Tea Party speakers demanded *both* that "government stay out of health care" and that "the government better not touch my Medicare." That is, these Tea Party activists wanted, valued, and were prepared to fight for Medicare—even though their ideology demanded that they engage in massive denial and refuse to see that Medicare is a government entitlement program. We hope that 20 or 30 years from now, in the next conservative backlash, the anti-government conservatives are demanding that the government not touch their free public higher education.

Conclusion: The University is Not For Sale

Our proposals are as out of the realm of possibility as were the national highway system, Medicare and Medicaid, civil rights for African-Americans, and universal elementary education when they were first proposed.

We are not proposing an outlandish agenda. California and New York City once offered tuition-free community college; the HOPE scholarships in the state of Georgia allow citizens of that state to attend public colleges and universities tuition-free; our veterans are rewarded for their service with a virtually free college education. We are proposing to universalize the best practices of our nation. We also have the advantage of the proof of history: the United States' half century of prosperity after World War II was anchored in the rise of the best public university system in the world. The next era of prosperity—real prosperity, not AIG, Lehman Brothers, Goldman Sachs, fake money prosperity—will also be built on a renewed investment in public universities.

But the aim of education is not just to stimulate economic growth and boost the free market. Students should not be "customers" or "clients" who are offered a "product" (an education or, at the very least, a diploma). We oppose a view that everything is for sale, that everything must make a profit, and that those "customers" with more money get more stuff.

> Unaddressed in that calculus is any question of what else an education might be for: to nurture critical thought; to expose individuals to the signal accomplishments of humankind; to develop in them an ability not just to listen actively but to respond intelligently.

> (Mead 2010)

College should not be only an 18–21-year-old's investment in a degree, but also for people of all ages to develop new capacities by studying and expanding human knowledge.

DISCUSSION QUESTIONS

1. Based on what decisions are actually made, *not* on rhetoric and public pronouncements, for your own institution, what do you think is the vision of higher education held by top administrators?
2. If our society made it a priority, could it afford to create a better but cheaper system of public higher education?
3. Would free public higher education for all be possible? If it were introduced, what would be its effects? How would it change your own choices and actions?
4. Why should people get higher education? What non-economic reasons (if any) are there to study at a college or university?

References

Acuff, Stewart, and Richard A. Levins. 2010. *Getting America Back to Work.* Minneapolis, MN: Tasora Books.

Ady, Robert M. 1997. "The Effects of State and Local Public Services on Economic Development." *New England Economic Review.* Federal Reserve of Boston, March/April.

American Association of University Professors. 2010. "The Annual Report on the Economic State of the Profession 2009–2010," *Academe,* March–April (96)2.

American Council on Education. 2008. "On the Pathway to the Presidency: Characteristics of Higher Education's Senior Leadership," Retrieved August 9, 2010 (http://www.cupahr.org/knowledge center/files/PathwayPresidency.pdf).

Angell, Marcia. 2004. *The Truth About the Drug Companies.* New York: Random House.

Association of Independent Colleges and Universities in Massachusetts. 2010. "AICUM Case Statement." January. Retrieved June 12, 2010(http://dcsclients.com/~aicum/PDF/AICUMCaseState mentJan2010.pdf).

Basken, Paul. 2008. "Spellings Sees Her Legacy Centering on 'Long Overdue' Assessment of Colleges." *Chronicle of Higher Education.* Retrieved December 12, 2008 (http://chronicle.com/daily/2008/12/8390n.htm).

Blumenstyk, Goldie. 2007. "Universities' Revenue from Licensing Patents Increases, Report Says. " *Chronicle of Higher Education* (December 4).

Bowen, William G., and Derek Bok. 2000. *The Shape of the River.* Princeton: Princeton University Press.

Bowen, William G., Matthew M. Chingos, and Michael S. McPherson. 2009. *Crossing the Finish Line: Completing College at America's Public Universities.* Princeton, NJ: Princeton University Press.

Brainard, Jeffrey, Paul Fain, and Kathryn Masterson. 2009. "Support-Staff Jobs Double in 20 Years, Outpacing Enrollment." *Chronicle of Higher Education* (April 24). Retrieved June 2, 2010(http://chronicle.com/weekly/v55/i33/33a00102.htm).

Brint, Steven. 1994. *In an Age of Experts.* Princeton, NJ: Princeton University Press.

Brint, Steven, and Jerome Karabel. 1989. *The Diverted Dream: Community Colleges and the Promise of Educational Opportunity in America, 1900–1985.* New York: Oxford University Press.

Brooks, David. 2008. "Stimulus for Skeptics." *New York Times* (28 October).

Center for the Study of Education Policy. 2010. *Grapevine: An Annual Compilation of Data on State Fiscal Support for Higher Education.* Retrieved June 12, 2010 (http://www.grapevine.ilstu.edu// historical).

Chait, Richard P. (ed.) 2002. *The Questions of Tenure*. Cambridge, MA: Harvard University Press.

Clawson, Dan. 2009. "Tenure and the Future of the University." *Science* 324 (#5931), May 29: 1147–48.

Cohen, Natalie. 2000. "American Capital Access." In *Business Location Decision-Making and the City: Bringing Companies Back*. Washington, DC: Brookings Institute.

College Board. 2009. "Trends in Student Aid." Retrieved June 12, 2010 (http://www.trends-collegeboard.com/student_aid).

Cross, John G., and Edie N. Goldenberg. 2009. *Off-Track Profs: Nontenured Teachers in Higher Education*. Cambridge, MA: MIT Press.

Current Population Reports. 2009. *Income, Poverty, and Health Insurance Coverage in the United States 2008*. Washington, DC: U.S. Census Bureau.

Current Population Survey. 2009. "Annual Social and Economic Supplement: Person Income." Retrieved June 12, 2010 (http://www.census.gov/hhes/www/cpstables/032009/perinc/toc.htm).

Dale, Stacey Berg, and James B. Krueger. 2002. "Estimating the Payoff to Attending a More Selective College: An Application of Selection on Observables and Unobservables." *Quarterly Journal of Economics* 117(4): 1491–527.

Dillon, Sam. 2007. "Troubles Grow for a University Built on Profits." *New York Times* (February 11). Retrieved June 12, 2010 (http://www.nytimes.com/2007/02/11/education/11phoenix.html?_r=1&adxnnl=1&adxnnlx=1274796239-fdQRKzscuUNH9lMOXt8yYw).

Eduventures. 2010. "From Survival to Sustainability: A Perspective on the State of Higher Education" (January). Retrieved June 18, 2010 (https://www1.vtrenz.net/imarkownerfiles/ownerassets/884/Eduventures%202009%20Summary%20Annual%20Report.pdf).

Folbre, Nancy. 2010. *Saving State U: Why We Must Fix Public Higher Education*. New York: The New Press.

Freidson, Eliot. 2001. *Professionalism: The Third Logic*. Chicago: University of Chicago Press.

Herman, Edward S. 1982. *The Real Terror Network: Terrorism in Fact and Propaganda*. Boston: South End Press.

Immerwahr, John. 1999. "Taking Responsibility: Leaders' Expectations of Higher Education" (January). National Center for Public Policy and Higher Education. Retrieved June 18, 2010 (http://www.highereducation.org/reports/responsibility/responsibility.shtml).

Inside Higher Ed. 2007. "Harvard's Aid Bonanza." (December 11). Retrieved June 12, 2010. (http://www.insidehighered.com/news/2007/12/11/harvard).

Kuhn, Thomas S. 1962. *The Structure of Scientific Revolutions*. Chicago: University of Chicago Press.

Larson, Magali Sarfati. 1977. *The Rise of Professionalism: A Sociological Analysis*. Berkeley: University of California Press.

Lee, John B. 1999. "How Do Students and Families Pay for College?" Pp. 9-27 in *Financing a College Education: How It Works, How It's Changing*, ed. Jacqueline E. King. Phoenix, AZ: The American Council on Education and Oryx Press.

Lieber, Ron. 2010. "Placing the Blame as Students are Buried in Debt." *New York Times* (28 May). Retrieved June 12, 2010 (http://www.nytimes.com/2010/05/29/your-money/student-loans/29money.html?scp=1&sq=student%20debt&st=cse).

Lindert, Peter H. 2004. *Growing Public: Social Spending and Economic Growth since the Eighteenth Century*. Two vols. New York: Cambridge University Press.

López-Rivera, Marisa. 2010. "Salaries of Senior Administrators Reflect Dip in Economy." *Chronicle of Higher Education* (21 February). Retrieved June 1, 2010 (http://chronicle.com/article/Salaries-of-Senior/64289).

Malanga, Steven. 2008. "Higher Ed Spending: Another Phony Stimulus?" Retrieved June 6, 2010 (http://www.manhattan-institute.org/html/miarticle.htm?id=3613).

Marklein, Mary Beth. 2009. "Four Year Colleges Graduate 53% of Students in 6 Years." *USA Today* (June 3). Retrieved June 12, 2010 (http://www.usatoday.com/news/education/2009-06-03-diploma-graduation-rate_N.htm).

Massachusetts Taxpayers Foundation. 2003. "State Spending More on Prisons than Higher Education." Bulletin of November 24. Retrieved November 18, 2006 (http://www.masstaxpayers.org/data/pdf/bulletins/11-24-03%20Corrections%20Bulletin.PDF).

Mead, Rebecca. 2010. "Learning by Degrees." *The New Yorker* (June 7). Retrieved June 7, 2010 (http://www.newyorker.com/talk/comment/2010/06/07/100607taco_talk_mead#ixzz0q6BIfPJI).

Mills, C. Wright. 1959. *The Sociological Imagination*. New York: Oxford University Press.

Mishel, Lawrence, Jared Bernstein, and Heidi Shierholz. 2009. *The State of Working America 2008/2009*. Ithaca, NY: Economic Policy Institute/ILR Press/Cornell University Press.

National Association of College and University Budget Officers. 2010. "U.S. and Canadian Institutions Listed by Fiscal Year 2009 Endowment Market Value." Retrieved June 12, 2010 (http://www.nacubo.org/Documents/research/2009_NCSE_Public_Tables_Endowment_Market_Values.pdf).

National Center for Education Statistics. 2004. *National Study of Postsecondary Faculty*. Retrieved June 13, 2010 (http://nces.ed.gov/pubs2005/2005172.pdf). Also previous years.

————. 2008. *Distance Education at Degree-Granting Postsecondary Institutions: 2006–07*. Retrieved June 12, 2010 (http://nces.ed.gov/fastfacts/display.asp?id=80).

————. 2010. *Digest of Education Statistics 2009*. Retrieved May 14, 2010 (http://nces.ed.gov/programs/digest/2009menu_tables.asp).

————. various years. *Digest of Education Statistics*. Retrieved Oct. 14, 2010 (http://nces.ed.gov/programs/digest).

National Center for Higher Education Management Systems. 2007. *Adding It Up: State Challenges for Increasing College Access and Success*. Retrieved June 12, 2010 (http://www.cpec.ca.gov/CompleteReports/ExternalDocuments/Adding_It_Up.pdf).

Owen, David. 1985. *None of the Above: Behind the Myth of Scholastic Aptitude*. Boston: Houghton Mifflin.

Penn State University Budget Office. 2010. "Total Budget and General Funds Budget 2008–09." Retrieved June 12, 2010 (http://www.budget.psu.edu/factbook/Finance2008/income200809.asp?Section=F).

Project on Student Debt. 2010. "Quick Facts about Student Debt." Retrieved June 12, 2010 (http://projectonstudentdebt.org/files/File/Debt_Facts_and_Sources.pdf).

Sacks, Peter. 2007. *Tearing Down the Gates: Confronting the Class Divide in American Education*. Berkeley: University of California Press.

Strout, Erin. 2006. "Administrators' Pay Rises 3.5 Percent, Beating Inflation for the Ninth Consecutive Year." *Chronicle of Higher Education*, 24 February, A28.

Swarthout, Luke. 2006. *Paying Back Not Giving Back: Student Debt's Negative Impact on Public Service Career Opportunities*. Retrieved June 12, 2010 (http://www.pirg.org/highered/payingback.pdf).

Tuchman, Gaye. 2009. *Wannabe U: Inside the Corporate University*. Chicago: University of Chicago Press.

U.S. Census Bureau. 1977. *Statistical Abstract of the United States: 1977*, 98th ed. Washington, DC. Retrieved May 30, 2010 (http://www.census.gov/statab/www).

———. 2009. *Statistical Abstract of the United States: 2010*, 129th ed. Washington, DC. Retrieved May 30, 2010 (http://www.census.gov/statab/www).

Washburn, Jennifer. 2005. *University Inc.: The Corporate Corruption of Higher Education*. New York: Basic Books.

Watts, Amy L. 2001. "Social Benefits of Going to College." *Education and the Common Good*. Retrieved June 12, 2010 (http://www.kltprc.net/books/educationcommongood/Chpt_04.htm).

Glossary/Index

2 year degrees 9–10

4 year degrees

    costs in 1970-1 of obtaining 24

    and debt accrued 34

    and graduating in 4 years 12, 36

    impact on income 13

A

ACT (originally American College Testing): standardized test taken by many students applying to college 12

administrators

    in business model 18, 21, 39, 40, 43, 46

    control over faculty hiring 21, 40, 43

    in faculty governance model 16–17, 39

    and increases in administrative support staff 39

    and problem of tenured faculty 39–40

    salaries 21, 43

admissions selectivity 11–12, 35

age of students 10

agency: a person's ability to make free choices and act on the basis of those choices. Agency and social structure are often paired: to what extent are a person's choices shaped by their place in the social structure, and to what extent by their individual actions? 3

American Dream 31

attendance, reasons for university 13

B

Bayh-Dole Act 1980 20

benchmarking 21

benefits of a higher education to individuals and society 13

British Petroleum (BP) 20
budget deficits 5
Bush, G.H.W. 5
Bush, G.W. 5
business model 18–20, 33, 45–46
    CEO administrator 18, 21, 39, 40, 43, 46
    contributing to rising costs of universities 26
    democratic alternative to 48–49
    and difficulty of tenured faculty in 39–40
    increases in administrative staff 39
    and preference for part-time low-paid staff 38, 40, 41, 43
    student recruitment 33

C
campus workers' pay and benefits 23, 38
chancellors and presidents
    average tenure 21
    in business model 18, 19, 21
    in faculty governance model 16, 17
China 1
class inequality 11, 26, 29, 35–36, 46
Clinton, Bill 5
community colleges 9–10
    state and parental funding 28
    teaching in 41, 42
contracting out work 38, 40
costs of universities and colleges
    decreasing government support 26–28, 48
    escalating for students and their families 23–24
    financial aid shifting from needs based to merit based 19, 29, 33
    and increased inequality 26
    market power pushing up 25
    and measures of success in business model 26
    reasons for escalating 25–29

D
debt, student 2, 34–35, 50
democratic alternative to business model 48–49
doctoral institutions 41

E

economic growth and correlation with investment in education 46, 52

endowments 28

enrollments 9

F

faculty

administrators' increased control over hiring 21, 40, 43

online courses 21, 40

part-time, low paid 38, 40, 41, 43

recruitment process 42–43

rise in non-tenured 40, 41, 43

salaries 21, 24–25, 40, 43

and student teaching 38, 41–42

see also **tenure**

faculty governance: a system in which faculty, operating through some organized body such as a Faculty Senate, have control over the basic decisions about education and research, such as what courses and majors are offered, as well as in shaping the general direction of the institution. Typically administrators, or the Board of Trustees, have the final say, but they traditionally do not go against a clear decision by the faculty. 16–18, 39

limitations of 48

fees and tuition 9, 23–24, 27, 28, 29, 50

financial aid

'high tuition–high aid' model 51

HOPE Scholarships, Georgia 52

Mass Grant 51

Pell grants 33–34

shift from 'needs based' to 'merit based' 19, 29, 33

financial industries 6

for-profit universities 10–11, 18, 34

free

higher education 49–52

school education 3, 50

funding

call for reversal of policies causing a lack of 47

crisis and effect on higher education system 11, 33, 45–46

decline of public sector 4, 21, 23, 27, 28

endowments 28

federal funding for research 20

for for-profit universities and colleges 10

for free higher education 51
internal allocations of 21
proportion of state to student's family 28, 50
public funding from 1960s to 2009 27
for research in a university as a business model 19–20
'self-funding' movement 27–28
state 50

G

gender equality 35
government
    budget deficits 5
    decline in funding for higher education 4, 21, 23, 27, 28
    decreasing support for higher education 26–27, 48
    financing of free higher education 50–51
    under neo-liberalism 5–6
    proportion of state to student's family funding 28, 50
    spending on education from 1960s to 2009 27
    tax cuts 5, 27, 47
graduation
    in 1970-1 24
    debt upon 2, 34–35, 50
    dropping out before 12, 34
    extra time needed for 3, 34
    jobs and income after 12–13
    likelihood of 12, 33, 35, 36
    from University of Phoenix 10
    US rates of 47

H

Harvard University 11, 25
    endowments 28
    graduating from 12
    Pell grants 34
    selection of admissions 11
    students from wealthy elite 12, 26
    test scores 12
    tuition and fees 23
health care expenditure 29
history of higher education 3–4
Holyoke Community College 11

on graduation from 12–13
graduation rate 12
professors' salaries 25
selection of admissions 12
state funding in 2010 27
test scores 12
tuition and fees 23
HOPE Scholarships, Georgia 52

I
income
average household 24
as a graduate 13
increasing inequality in 26, 47
stagnation of 47
inequality
class 11, 26, 29, 35–36, 46
in higher education 31–37, 46
increasing income 26, 47
investment in education and correlation with economic growth 46, 52

K
Kuhn, Thomas 45

M
Mann, Horace 3, 50
market power of universities and colleges 25–29
Mass Grant 51
Mead, Rebecca 52
Medicare 51–52
military spending 5–6
Mills, C. Wright 2
Morrill Act 1862 3–4

N
neo-liberal: the political view that "the free market" is the best way to organize and manage social arrangements, and that the government is a problem and should be reduced, both in size and in its power to regulate 5, 5–7, 18, 23, 27, 45
Novartis 20
numbers of students 8–9
1960s and 70s 4

O

Obama, Barack 1, 5, 50

online courses
    and contracting out of faculty 21, 40
    and failure to graduate from 34
    growth in 10–11
    at University of Phoenix 10

out-of-state students 19, 23

P

part-time
    staff 38, 40, 41, 43
    students 10, 12

patents 20

Patrick, Deval 1

pay for campus workers 23, 38

Pell grants 33–34

Pennsylvania State University 27–28

Pikeville College 11
    graduation rate 12
    professors' salaries 25
    selection of admissions 11–12
    test scores 12
    tuition and fees 23

Porter, Michael 47

post-baccalaureate education 9

presidents and chancellors
    average tenure 21
    in business model 18, 19, 21
    in faculty governance model 16, 17

prison expenditure 28–29

private colleges and universities
    endowments 28
    enrollments 9
    financial aid for students 29
    growth of 4
    not-for profit 10
    online courses 11

privatization (privatized): a political outlook that believes in having services traditionally provided by the government through general taxes-such as highways, buses, and subways, primary schools, and public universities-paid for by individuals and provided by private, for-profit companies. The belief, not borne out by evidence, is that for-profit companies will provide similar quality services for less cost. The result has generally been lower quality, less accountability, and a transfer of money from taxpayers to for-profit companies. 6

professionalism: a system that provides considerable respect for, and autonomy to, a set of experts, whose expertise is based on education and training, and who are believed to be governed by values and commitments to a higher social good, rather than simply to their own privilege and advancement 16

professors 24, 25, 41, 46

provosts 21

public colleges and universities 3–4
    endowments 28
    enrollments 9
    financial aid to students 19, 29, 33
    growth of 4
    not-for profit 10
    not viewed as a 'right' 27
    'self-funding' movement for 27–28

public school movement 3

R

race equality 35

ranking system 21, 26, 33, 34

Reagan, Ronald 5, 29, 40–41

recruitment processes 42–43

research
    community involvement in deciding upon 48
    federal funding for 20
    funding in a university as a business model 19–20
    grants 26
    and tenure 16
    University of California, Berkeley funding 20

S

salaries
    of administrators 21, 43
    faculty 21, 24–25, 40, 43

SAT (Scholastic Aptitude Test): standardized test taken by many students applying to college 12

    corresponding with class and income 26
    merit based aid dependent on 29

and national rankings 26, 33
scholarship 16, 48
selection of admissions 11–12, 35
Social Security taxes 51
social structure: a set of arrangements, usually embodied in institutions but going beyond any particular organization, that shapes our behavior and leads us to do certain things, and not to do other things. Where you are located in a social structure determines what is expected of you and what privileges you are accorded. Anyone occupying a similar place in that social structure will tend to behave similarly. 2
society benefits from higher education 13
The Sociological Imagination 2
sociological imagination: the ability to see the relations between personal problems and the larger society, the ways in which what seem to be personal issues are also public issues of the social structure 2–3
Spellings, Margaret 1
The Structure of Scientific Revolutions 45
students
  in 1970–1 24
  age of 10
  benefits of a higher education for 13
  as consumers 18–19, 48
  a democratic voice in running of university 48
  enrollments 9
  graduation rates in US 47
  low-income 33, 34, 35, 36, 46, 51
  numbers of 4, 8–9
  out-of-state 19, 23
  part-time students 10, 12
  reasons for obtaining a higher education 13
  teaching of 38, 41–42

T
tax cuts 5, 27, 47
Taxol 20
tenure: an award, granted to some faculty at the end of their sixth year, that protects faculty from being fired for expressing unpopular views. Tenured faculty can be fired if they commit crimes or fail to perform their basic duties, but (supposedly) not for the positions they take on controversial issues, no matter how outrageous colleagues, the public, administrators, or politicians consider those views. Tenure-system faculty who are not granted tenure in their sixth year are fired. 16–17, 39–40

advantages of 41–42
arguments against 39–40
assaults on 40
decline in tenure-track faculty 41, 42
as a means to recruit accomplished people 40
recruitment process for 43
salaries 21, 24–25, 40, 43
and student teaching 38
tuition and fees 9, 23–24, 27, 28, 29, 50

U

University of California Berkeley 20
University of Massachusetts Agricultural College 4
University of Massachusetts Amherst 11
graduation rate 12
Pell grants 34
professors' salaries 25
selection of admissions 11
state funding in 2010 27
student payments exceeding state payments in 2010 28
test scores 12
tuition and fees 23, 28
University of Michigan 28, 34
University of Phoenix 10
University of Texas 28
University of Wisconsin 4, 34

W

Wal-Marted: having followed a set of employment and organizational practices that are attributed to Wal-Mart-hiring workers at low wages, preferring part-time to fulltime workers, providing minimal benefits and making it difficult to qualify for even those benefits, and, wherever possible, replacing employees of the organization with employees of a sub-contractor. The competition among sub-contractors leads them to follow low-wage policies in order to win the contract; if sub-contractors are caught in legal or moral violations, the central organization can insist the legal violation is exclusively the fault of the sub-contractor, and has nothing to do with the central organization 38
Washburn, Jennifer 20